Conference of the North American Chapter of the Association for Computational Linguistics (NAACL 2024)

Languages of Latin America

Tutorial Abstracts

Mexico City, Mexico
16-21 June 2024

ISBN: 978-1-7138-9897-9

Printed from e-media with permission by:

Curran Associates, Inc.
57 Morehouse Lane
Red Hook, NY 12571

CURRAN ASSOCIATES INC. proceedings.com

Some format issues inherent in the e-media version may also appear in this print version.

Association for Computational Linguistics
209 N. Eighth Street
Stroudsburg, Pennsylvania 18360

Phone: 1-570-476-8006
Fax: 1-570-476-0860

acl@aclweb.org

Additional copies of this publication are available from:

Curran Associates, Inc.
57 Morehouse Lane
Red Hook, NY 12571 USA
Phone: 845-758-0400
Fax: 845-758-2633
Email: curran@proceedings.com
Web: www.proceedings.com

NAACL 2024

The 2024 Conference of the North American Chapter of the Association for Computational Linguistics

Proceedings of the Tutorial Abstracts

June 16-21, 2024

Introduction

Welcome to the tutorial session of NAACL 2024!

We are delighted to have you join us for this year's NAACL tutorial session, a cornerstone event of our conference. Our tutorials are designed to provide attendees with a comprehensive introduction to a diverse array of cutting-edge and emerging topics, delivered by esteemed researchers who are leaders in their fields. These sessions aim to equip you with the latest insights, tools, and methodologies, enhancing your understanding of the dynamic landscape of computational linguistics and natural language processing.

This year follows the tradition: the call, submission, reviewing, and selection of tutorials were coordinated jointly for EACL, NAACL, ACL, and EMNLP. We formed a review committee including the EACL tutorial chairs (Sharid Loáiciga, Mohsen Mesgar), NAACL tutorial chairs (Rui Zhang, Nathan Schneider, Snigdha Chaturvedi), ACL tutorial chairs (Luis Chiruzzo, Hung-yi Lee, Leonardo Ribeiro), and the interim EMNLP tutorial chair (Isabelle Augenstein). Each tutorial proposal was meticulously reviewed by a panel of three reviewers, who evaluated the submissions based on a range of criteria. The selection criteria included clarity and preparedness, novelty or timely character of the topic, instructors' experience, likely audience interest, open access to the teaching materials, diversity (multilingualism, gender, age, and geolocation), and the compatibility of preferred venues. A total of 27 tutorial submissions were received, and 6 were selected for presentation at NAACL. These tutorials promise to deliver engaging and informative sessions that cater to a wide range of interests and expertise levels within our community.

We extend our heartfelt gratitude to all tutorial authors for their contributions and to the conference organizers for their unwavering commitment and dedicated collaboration, particularly General Chair Katrin Erk.

We sincerely hope that you find these tutorials enriching and that they enhance your conference experience. Enjoy the tutorials and the many opportunities for learning and networking at NAACL 2024!

Warm regards,
NAACL 2024 Tutorial Co-Chairs,
Rui Zhang
Nathan Schneider
Snigdha Chaturvedi

Organizing Committee

General Chair

Katrin Erk, The University of Texas at Austin

Program Chairs

Kevin Duh, Johns Hopkins University
Helena Gomez, Universidad Nacional Autónoma de México
Steven Bethard, University of Arizona

Tutorial Chairs

Rui Zhang, Penn State University
Nathan Schneider, Georgetown University
Snigdha Chaturvedi, UNC-Chapel Hill

Table of Contents

Catch Me If You GPT: Tutorial on Deepfake Texts

Adaku Uchendu[†] **Saranya Venkatraman** **Thai Le**[♠] **Dongwon Lee**

MIT Lincoln Laboratory, Lexington, MA, USA[†]
The Pennsylvania State University, University Park, PA, USA
Indiana University, Bloomington, IN, USA[♠]

adaku.uchendu@ll.mit.edu[†], {saranyav, dongwon}@psu.edu, leqthai.vn@gmail.com[♠]

Abstract

In recent years, Natural Language Generation (NLG) techniques have greatly advanced, especially in the realm of Large Language Models (LLMs). With respect to the quality of generated texts, it is no longer trivial to tell the difference between human-written and LLM-generated texts (i.e., deepfake texts). While this is a celebratory feat for NLG, it poses new security risks (e.g., the generation of misinformation). To combat this novel challenge, researchers have developed diverse techniques to detect deepfake texts. While this niche field of *deepfake text detection* is growing, the field of NLG is growing at a much faster rate, thus making it difficult to understand the complex interplay between state-of-the-art NLG methods and the detectability of their generated texts. To understand such inter-play, two new computational problems emerge: (1) *Deepfake Text Attribution* (DTA) and (2) *Deepfake Text Obfuscation* (DTO) problems, where the DTA problem is concerned with attributing the authorship of a given text to one of k NLG methods, while the DTO problem is to evade the authorship of a given text by modifying parts of the text. In this **cutting-edge tutorial**, therefore, we call attention to the serious security risk both emerging problems pose and give a comprehensive review of recent literature on the detection and obfuscation of deepfake text authorships. Our tutorial will be 3 hours long with *a mix of lecture and hands-on examples* for interactive audience participation. You can find our tutorial materials here: `https://tinyurl.com/naacl24-tutorial`.

1 Introduction

Since the advent of the Transformer network architecture (Vaswani et al., 2017) in 2018, the field of NLG has exponentially expanded. This architectural design led to the development of GPT-1 (Radford et al., 2018), the first installment in deepfake text generative models that are capable of generating long-coherent texts. Since then there have been several (i.e., GPT-4 (OpenAI, 2023), Flan-T5 (Chung et al., 2022), LlaMA (Meta, 2023), etc). In fact, with each new installment in the world of long-coherent text generation, these generated texts become more and more human-like. Such LLM-generated texts are referred to as **deepfake texts**. While this is a great feat for the field of NLG and has several impactful applications, such text generators pose a security risk. This security risk is the potential inability to distinguish human-written texts from deepfake texts, which allows for malicious users of such NLG models to generate misinformation (Zellers et al., 2019; Uchendu et al., 2020), and propaganda (Varol et al., 2017).

Therefore, we have 2 problems to tackle - (1) distinguish deepfake texts from human-written texts, and (2) detect obfuscated (i.e., a technique to evade detection) deepfake texts. While several researchers are working on these two problems, a few issues with deepfake text generation have been highlighted by other researchers. These issues or limitations include: (1) memorization & plagiarizing of training set (Carlini et al., 2021; Duskin et al., 2021; Lee et al., 2022), (2) generation of toxic & harmful speech (Pavlopoulos et al., 2020; Venkit et al., 2023; Deshpande et al., 2023), (3) generation of hallucinated text (Zhou et al., 2021; Ji et al., 2023), (4) generation of misinformation (Jawahar et al., 2020; Pan et al., 2023; Shevlane et al., 2023), etc.

Such limitations of deepfake text generators, further confirm the need to reliably distinguish human-written and deepfake texts. Thus, in this tutorial, we explore the following: (1) Deepfake Text Attribution (DTA) which involves correctly attributing the authorship of a given text to one of k NLG methods, and (2) Deepfake Text Obfuscation (DTO) that focus on evading the authorship of a given text by modifying parts of the text.

Proceedings of the 2024 Conference of the North American Chapter of the Association for Computational Linguistics: Human Language Technologies (Volume 5: Tutorial Abstracts), pages 1–7
June 16-21, 2024 ©2024 Association for Computational Linguistics

2 Target Audience & Prerequisites

The target audience includes graduate students, practitioners, and researchers attending the NAACL conference, coming from different areas of the Machine Learning (ML)/Natural Language Processing (NLP)/Computational Linguistics (CL) field. Basic common knowledge in NLP and ML would be helpful but not required. We plan to make the tutorial as self-contained as possible for a wider audience. We expect about 50-70 participants to attend our tutorial. Lastly, we believe that this tutorial will be most suited to the NAACL 2024 conference.

3 Tutorial Type

Hence, we propose a **cutting-edge** tutorial with hands-on examples that will present the current research on *deepfake text detection*. Our tutorial will be mainly **a mix of lecture and hands-on style**. It will include examples of the generation, detection, and obfuscation of deepfake texts for interactive participation from the audience.

4 Tutorial Outline

The materials of our tutorial will mainly contain lecture-based slideshows of this **cutting-edge** niche field. Although we are delivering the tutorial in lecture style, we also include a few quick interactive activities to showcase real-life examples of deepfake texts and their implications. They will be polls, binary/multiple-choice, and group-based questions.

4.1 Introduction and Background (30 minutes)

This section will introduce the topic of NLG and the many improvements it has seen since the incorporation of the Transformer network into Language models. After this introduction, we will briefly discuss deepfake text generation. Next, we motivate the many benefits of deepfake texts as well as the risks they could pose. This will allow us to transition to briefly introducing the main problem - *deepfake text attribution and obfuscation*. Finally, we provide an outline of the tutorial which will include topics that would be covered and not covered in the tutorial.

Then, we will focus on the evolution of deepfake text generation and detection. We will also briefly introduce the history of Deepfake Text Attribution (DTA) and Deepfake Text Obfuscation (DTO). Particularly, we will discuss the different terminologies used to describe deepfake texts (such as artificial texts, synthetic texts, machine-generated texts, etc.). As this is still a relatively new field, there is still no agreed-upon universal term for deepfake text generation. We will also briefly highlight why we use the term *deepfake texts generation*, instead of the other terms.

4.2 Deepfake Text Attribution (40 minutes)

This section will present the following sub-topics:

1. **Interactive Activity.** We start this session by inviting the audience to join in a hands-on activity. The attendees will be asked to detect some examples of human-written v.s. deepfake texts. We will prepare paper handouts for the audience for this activity, which will include all the needed descriptions. In the hybrid setting, we will show the material through the provided video call system (e.g., Zoom). Through this activity, we want the attendees to grasp the difficulty of detecting deepfake texts, due to the challenges of distinguishing them from human-written ones.

2. **Datasets.** We will introduce several relevant publicly available English and multilingual datasets across different domains such as TuringBench dataset (Uchendu et al., 2021), M4 (Wang et al., 2023), Med-MMHL (Sun et al., 2023), DeepfakeTextDetect (Li et al., 2023), etc.

3. **Computational Approaches.** We will present the different ways in which researchers have tackled the problem of deepfake text detection. We will also discuss the limitations of the current computational approaches and potential ways the ML/NLP/CL communities could mitigate or solve such limitations. Some of the current SOTA automated DTA approaches include GPT-2 Output Detector[1], DetectGPT (Mitchell et al., 2023), GPTZero[2], etc.

4. **Human Approaches.** We will present and discuss the several ways in which researchers have attempted to improve human detection

[1] https://huggingface.co/spaces/openai/openai-detector

[2] https://gptzero.me/

(Clark et al., 2021; Ippolito et al., 2020; Dugan et al., 2020; Pillutla et al., 2021; Gehrmann et al., 2019; Dou et al., 2021; Uchendu et al., 2023b; Perkins et al., 2023) of deepfake texts.

4.3 Watermarking LLMs (25 minutes)

In addition, we will discuss several watermarking techniques (Kirchenbauer et al., 2023; Yoo et al., 2023; Zhao et al., 2023), another computational approach to mitigating the potential negative effects of deepfake text generation. Watermarking essentially embeds a hidden pattern into a text such that the pattern enables its detection by deepfake text detectors while being imperceptible to the human eye. This has implications for inhibiting misuse, misattribution and Intellectual Property (IP) infringement of deepfake texts, and is a growing and increasingly crucial line of work for the safe and large-scale deployment of LLMs in real-world settings.

4.4 QUESTIONS (10 minutes)

4.5 BREAK (30 minutes)

4.6 Obfuscation of Deepfake Texts (40 minutes)

This section will present the following sub-topics:

1. **Deepfake Text Obfuscation Techniques.** We first introduce the definitions of DTO task and how it is different from adversarial attacks. Then, we will briefly describe some of the current SOTA DTO algorithms (e.g., (Mahmood et al., 2019; Haroon et al., 2021)) and also some relevant adversarial attack techniques on text. Then, we discuss in detail all the research that has been done in this area to highlight the lack of adversarial robustness of SOTA DTA models for deepfake texts detection (Jun et al., 2022; Crothers et al., 2022; Gagiano et al., 2021; Wolff and Wolff, 2020). Next, we discuss the gaps in the literature, the future direction of problems in this domain, and the ways in which the ML, NLP and CL community could contribute and improve upon the current landscape.

2. **Interactive Game.** We will demonstrate a demo for adversarially perturbing the deepfake texts in real-time to mislead the deepfake texts DTA detectors to misclassify. For this demonstration, we will utilize the ChatGPT Detectors - GPTZero, and ZeroGPT.

4.7 Applications and Implications (15 minutes)

We will use this session to encourage the audience to ponder how deepfake texts will influence their sub-discipline community. In particular, we will discuss how improvements in *DTA and DTO tasks* could be applied to similar problems like *fake news detection, hallucinated text detection, chatbot detection, hate speech detection*, etc. We will also briefly discuss conversational AI models, such as ChatGPT under the context of the tutorial (e.g., distinguishing between human and automated conversational agents via DTA). Finally, we will then focus our talk on discussing one to two specific scenarios where deepfake texts can be utilized for both good and malicious purposes. We will encourage the audience to engage in the discussion via live polling.

4.8 Future Direction (10 minutes)

In this section, we will present and discuss the future directions in this field and potential ways the ML, NLP, and CL communities can both benefit and assist. These directions include the building of (1) *explainable & Intuitive DTA models for deepfake text detection*, (2) *robust style-based classifier*, and (3) *deepfake text obfuscation for $k > 2$ authors*.

4.9 QUESTIONS (15 minutes)

5 Reading List

The references included in this tutorial proposal are relevant references to help the audience get more acquainted with the topic. Also, this NAACL 2024 tutorial will be largely drawn from the authors' recent survey paper (Uchendu et al., 2023a).

6 Tutors

Presenters of this tutorial include a diverse group of researchers. See below for their brief biographies.

- **Adaku Uchendu**[3] is a Technical Staff member (AI researcher) at MIT Lincoln Lab. She recently earned her Ph.D. in Information Sciences and Technology from Penn State University. She was a Sloan scholarship fellow, an NSF CyberCorps SFS scholar, and a Button-Waller fellow. Her dissertation is titled *Reverse Turing Test in the Age of Deepfake Texts*. She has authored several papers

[3]Main Contact

in deepfake text detection at top-tier conferences & journals - EMNLP, KDD Exploration, Web Conference, AAAI HCOMP, NAACL, etc. In addition, she led two similar Tutorials titled, *Tutorial on Artificial Text Detection* (Uchendu et al., 2022) at the INLG conference in July 2022 and *Catch Me If You GAN: Generation, Detection, and Obfuscation of Deepfake Texts* (Fionda et al., 2023) at the Web conference in April 2023. Also, she will give a similar tutorial (with the same title as this proposal) at the 2023 NSF Cybersecurity Summit in October 2023. More details of her research can be found at: https://adauchendu.github.io/.
E-mail: adaku.uchendu@ll.mit.edu

- **Saranya Venkatraman** is a Ph.D. student at Penn State University, working under the guidance of Dr. Dongwon Lee in the College of Information Sciences and Technology. Her research focuses on using psycholinguistics theories and theories of human cognition to inform natural language processing techniques, with a focus on deepfake text detection and deepfake text obfuscation. She also contributed to and presented a *Tutorial on Artificial Text Detection* (Uchendu et al., 2022) at the INLG conference, in July 2022 and has published in top-tier conferences like AAAI, EMNLP, EACL, NAACL, and CHI. More details of her research can be found at: https://saranya-venkatraman.github.io/.
E-mail: saranyav@psu.edu

- **Thai Le** is joining the Department of Computer Science at Indiana University as an Assistant Professor. He has been an Assistant Professor at the University of Mississippi, worked at Amazon Alexa, and obtained his doctorate from The Pennsylvania State University. He has published several relevant works at top-tier conferences such as KDD, ICDM, ACL, EMNLP, and Web Conference. He is also one of the Instructors in a similar Tutorial presented at the Web conference in April 2023 and the 2023 NSF Cybersecurity Summit in October 2023. In general, he researches the trustworthiness of machine learning and AI, with a focus on explainability and adversarial robustness of machine learning models. More details of his research can be found at: https://lethaiq.github.io/tql3.
E-mail: leqthai.vn@gmail.com

- **Dongwon Lee** is a Full Professor in the College of Information Sciences and Technology (a.k.a. iSchool) at Penn State University, and also an ACM Distinguished Scientist and Fulbright Cyber Security Scholar. Before starting at Penn State, he worked at AT&T Bell Labs and obtained his Ph.D. in Computer Science from UCLA. From 2015 to 2017, he also served as a Program Director at National Science Foundation (NSF), co-managing cybersecurity education and research programs and contributing to the development of national research priorities. In general, he researches problems in the areas of data science, machine learning, and cybersecurity. Since 2017, in particular, he has led the SysFake project at Penn State, investigating computational and socio-technical solutions to better combat fake news. More details of his research can be found at: http://pike.psu.edu. Previously, he has given nine tutorials at various venues, including WWW, AAAI, CIKM, SDM, ICDE, and WebSci.
E-mail: dongwon@psu.edu

7 Previous Tutorials

Adaku, Thai, and Dongwon presented a similar tutorial at the *ACM Web conference* in April 2023, titled "Catch Me If You GAN: Generation, Detection, and Obfuscation of Deepfake Texts"[4]. Furthermore, the tutors led the same tutorial at the *2023 NSF Cybersecurity Summit* in October 2023. However, due to the growing interest in *deepfake text detection*, and the emerging strategies to ascertain the authorship of deepfake texts, we introduce another tutor, Saranya Venkatraman for the NAACL Tutorial to include latest developments, such as watermarking strategies of deepfake texts both in theory and practical applications.

8 Ethics Statement

While we highlight the potential negative applications of LLMs to motivate the creation of solutions to mitigate their effects, we understand that malevolent actors could use such knowledge maliciously.

[4] https://adauchendu.github.io/Tutorials/

However, since the focus of our tutorial is on mitigation, we believe that the benefits of this tutorial outweigh the risks. Additionally, our tutorial will also include strategies, like watermarking that can be used by creators of LLMs to further mitigate the potential negative exploitation of LLMs.

References

Nicholas Carlini, Florian Tramer, Eric Wallace, Matthew Jagielski, Ariel Herbert-Voss, Katherine Lee, Adam Roberts, Tom Brown, Dawn Song, Ulfar Erlingsson, et al. 2021. Extracting training data from large language models. In *30th USENIX Security Symposium (USENIX Security 21)*, pages 2633–2650.

Hyung Won Chung, Le Hou, Shayne Longpre, Barret Zoph, Yi Tay, William Fedus, Eric Li, Xuezhi Wang, Mostafa Dehghani, Siddhartha Brahma, et al. 2022. Scaling instruction-finetuned language models. *arXiv preprint arXiv:2210.11416*.

Elizabeth Clark, Tal August, Sofia Serrano, Nikita Haduong, Suchin Gururangan, and Noah A Smith. 2021. All that's 'human'is not gold: Evaluating human evaluation of generated text. In *Proceedings of the 59th Annual Meeting of the Association for Computational Linguistics and the 11th International Joint Conference on Natural Language Processing (Volume 1: Long Papers)*, pages 7282–7296.

Evan Crothers, Nathalie Japkowicz, Herna Viktor, and Paula Branco. 2022. Adversarial robustness of neural-statistical features in detection of generative transformers. *arXiv preprint arXiv:2203.07983*.

Ameet Deshpande, Vishvak Murahari, Tanmay Rajpurohit, Ashwin Kalyan, and Karthik Narasimhan. 2023. Toxicity in chatgpt: Analyzing persona-assigned language models. *arXiv preprint arXiv:2304.05335*.

Yao Dou, Maxwell Forbes, Rik Koncel-Kedziorski, Noah A Smith, and Yejin Choi. 2021. Scarecrow: A framework for scrutinizing machine text. *arXiv preprint arXiv:2107.01294*.

Liam Dugan, Daphne Ippolito, Arun Kirubarajan, and Chris Callison-Burch. 2020. Roft: A tool for evaluating human detection of machine-generated text. In *Proceedings of the 2020 Conference on Empirical Methods in Natural Language Processing: System Demonstrations*, pages 189–196.

Kayla Duskin, Shivam Sharma, Ji Young Yun, Emily Saldanha, and Dustin Arendt. 2021. Evaluating and explaining natural language generation with genx. In *Proceedings of the Second Workshop on Data Science with Human in the Loop: Language Advances*, pages 70–78.

Valeria Fionda, Olaf Hartig, Reyhaneh Abdolazimi, Sihem Amer-Yahia, Hongzhi Chen, Xiao Chen, Peng Cui, Jeffrey Dalton, Xin Luna Dong, Lisette Espin-Noboa, et al. 2023. Tutorials at the web conference 2023. In *Companion Proceedings of the ACM Web Conference 2023*, pages 648–658.

Rinaldo Gagiano, Maria Myung-Hee Kim, Xiuzhen Jenny Zhang, and Jennifer Biggs. 2021. Robustness analysis of grover for machine-generated news detection. In *Proceedings of the The 19th Annual Workshop of the Australasian Language Technology Association*, pages 119–127.

Sebastian Gehrmann, Hendrik Strobelt, and Alexander M Rush. 2019. Gltr: Statistical detection and visualization of generated text. In *Proceedings of the 57th Annual Meeting of the Association for Computational Linguistics: System Demonstrations*, pages 111–116.

Muhammad Haroon, Fareed Zaffar, Padmini Srinivasan, and Zubair Shafiq. 2021. Avengers ensemble! improving transferability of authorship obfuscation. *arXiv preprint arXiv:2109.07028*.

Daphne Ippolito, Daniel Duckworth, Chris Callison-Burch, and Douglas Eck. 2020. Automatic detection of generated text is easiest when humans are fooled. In *Proceedings of the 58th Annual Meeting of the Association for Computational Linguistics*, pages 1808–1822.

Ganesh Jawahar, Muhammad Abdul-Mageed, and VS Laks Lakshmanan. 2020. Automatic detection of machine generated text: A critical survey. In *Proceedings of the 28th International Conference on Computational Linguistics*, pages 2296–2309.

Ziwei Ji, Nayeon Lee, Rita Frieske, Tiezheng Yu, Dan Su, Yan Xu, Etsuko Ishii, Ye Jin Bang, Andrea Madotto, and Pascale Fung. 2023. Survey of hallucination in natural language generation. *ACM Computing Surveys*, 55(12):1–38.

Evan Lim Hong Jun, Chong Wen Haw, and Chieu Hai Leong. 2022. Robustness analysis of neural text detectors.

John Kirchenbauer, Jonas Geiping, Yuxin Wen, Jonathan Katz, Ian Miers, and Tom Goldstein. 2023. A watermark for large language models. *arXiv preprint arXiv:2301.10226*.

Jooyoung Lee, Thai Le, Jinghui Chen, and Dongwon Lee. 2022. Do language models plagiarize? *arXiv preprint arXiv:2203.07618*.

Yafu Li, Qintong Li, Leyang Cui, Wei Bi, Longyue Wang, Linyi Yang, Shuming Shi, and Yue Zhang. 2023. Deepfake text detection in the wild. *arXiv preprint arXiv:2305.13242*.

Asad Mahmood, Faizan Ahmad, Zubair Shafiq, Padmini Srinivasan, and Fareed Zaffar. 2019. A girl has no name: Automated authorship obfuscation using mutant-x. *Proc. Priv. Enhancing Technol.*, 2019(4):54–71.

AI Meta. 2023. Introducing llama: A foundational, 65-billion-parameter large language model. *Meta AI. https://ai. facebook. com/blog/large-language-model-llama-meta-ai.*

Eric Mitchell, Yoonho Lee, Alexander Khazatsky, Christopher D Manning, and Chelsea Finn. 2023. Detectgpt: Zero-shot machine-generated text detection using probability curvature. *arXiv preprint arXiv:2301.11305.*

OpenAI. 2023. Gpt-4 technical report.

Yikang Pan, Liangming Pan, Wenhu Chen, Preslav Nakov, Min-Yen Kan, and William Yang Wang. 2023. On the risk of misinformation pollution with large language models. *arXiv preprint arXiv:2305.13661.*

John Pavlopoulos, Jeffrey Sorensen, Lucas Dixon, Nithum Thain, and Ion Androutsopoulos. 2020. Toxicity detection: Does context really matter? In *Proceedings of the 58th Annual Meeting of the Association for Computational Linguistics*, pages 4296–4305.

Mike Perkins, Jasper Roe, Darius Postma, James McGaughran, and Don Hickerson. 2023. Game of tones: Faculty detection of gpt-4 generated content in university assessments. *arXiv preprint arXiv:2305.18081.*

Krishna Pillutla, Swabha Swayamdipta, Rowan Zellers, John Thickstun, Sean Welleck, Yejin Choi, and Zaid Harchaoui. 2021. An information divergence measure between neural text and human text. *arXiv preprint arXiv:2102.01454.*

Alec Radford, Karthik Narasimhan, Tim Salimans, Ilya Sutskever, et al. 2018. Improving language understanding by generative pre-training.

Toby Shevlane, Sebastian Farquhar, Ben Garfinkel, Mary Phuong, Jess Whittlestone, Jade Leung, Daniel Kokotajlo, Nahema Marchal, Markus Anderljung, Noam Kolt, et al. 2023. Model evaluation for extreme risks. *arXiv preprint arXiv:2305.15324.*

Yanshen Sun, Jianfeng He, Shuo Lei, Limeng Cui, and Chang-Tien Lu. 2023. Med-mmhl: A multi-modal dataset for detecting human-and llm-generated misinformation in the medical domain. *arXiv preprint arXiv:2306.08871.*

Adaku Uchendu, Thai Le, and Dongwon Lee. 2023a. Attribution and obfuscation of neural text authorship: A data mining perspective. *SIGKDD Explorations*, page vol. 25.

Adaku Uchendu, Thai Le, Kai Shu, and Dongwon Lee. 2020. Authorship attribution for neural text generation. In *Proceedings of the 2020 Conference on Empirical Methods in Natural Language Processing (EMNLP)*, pages 8384–8395.

Adaku Uchendu, Jooyoung Lee, Hua Shen, Thai Le, Ting-Hao 'Kenneth' Huang, and Dongwon Lee. 2023b. Does human collaboration enhance the accuracy of identifying llm-generated deepfake texts? *The Eleventh AAAI Conference on Human Computation and Crowdsourcing.*

Adaku Uchendu, Zeyu Ma, Thai Le, Rui Zhang, and Dongwon Lee. 2021. Turingbench: A benchmark environment for turing test in the age of neural text generation. In *Findings of the Association for Computational Linguistics: EMNLP 2021*, pages 2001–2016.

Adaku Uchendu, Vladislav Mikhailov, Jooyoung Lee, Saranya Venkatraman, Tatiana Shavrina, and Ekaterina Artemova. 2022. Tutorial on artificial text detection. *15th International Conference on Natural Language Generation (INLG): Tutorial.*

Onur Varol, Emilio Ferrara, Clayton Davis, Filippo Menczer, and Alessandro Flammini. 2017. Online human-bot interactions: Detection, estimation, and characterization. In *Proceedings of the international AAAI conference on web and social media*, volume 11, pages 280–289.

Ashish Vaswani, Noam Shazeer, Niki Parmar, Jakob Uszkoreit, Llion Jones, Aidan N Gomez, Łukasz Kaiser, and Illia Polosukhin. 2017. Attention is all you need. *Advances in neural information processing systems*, 30.

Pranav Narayanan Venkit, Sanjana Gautam, Ruchi Panchanadikar, Ting-Hao Huang, and Shomir Wilson. 2023. Nationality bias in text generation. In *Proceedings of the 17th Conference of the European Chapter of the Association for Computational Linguistics*, pages 116–122.

Yuxia Wang, Jonibek Mansurov, Petar Ivanov, Jinyan Su, Artem Shelmanov, Akim Tsvigun, Chenxi Whitehouse, Osama Mohammed Afzal, Tarek Mahmoud, Alham Fikri Aji, et al. 2023. M4: Multi-generator, multi-domain, and multi-lingual black-box machine-generated text detection. *arXiv preprint arXiv:2305.14902.*

Max Wolff and Stuart Wolff. 2020. Attacking neural text detectors. *arXiv preprint arXiv:2002.11768.*

KiYoon Yoo, Wonhyuk Ahn, Jiho Jang, and Nojun Kwak. 2023. Robust multi-bit natural language watermarking through invariant features. In *Proceedings of the 61st Annual Meeting of the Association for Computational Linguistics (Volume 1: Long Papers)*, pages 2092–2115.

Rowan Zellers, Ari Holtzman, Hannah Rashkin, Yonatan Bisk, Ali Farhadi, Franziska Roesner, and Yejin Choi. 2019. Defending against neural fake news. In *Advances in Neural Information Processing Systems.*

Xuandong Zhao, Yu-Xiang Wang, and Lei Li. 2023. Protecting language generation models via invisible watermarking. *arXiv preprint arXiv:2302.03162.*

Chunting Zhou, Graham Neubig, Jiatao Gu, Mona Diab, Francisco Guzmán, Luke Zettlemoyer, and Marjan Ghazvininejad. 2021. Detecting hallucinated content in conditional neural sequence generation. In *Findings of the Joint Conference of the 59th Annual Meeting of the Association for Computational Linguistics and the 11th International Joint Conference on Natural Language Processing (ACL-IJCNLP Findings)*, Virtual.

Combating Security and Privacy Issues in the Era of Large Language Models

Muhao Chen[†] **Chaowei Xiao**[‡⋆] **Huan Sun**[◇] **Lei Li**[♠] **Leon Derczynski**[♣] **Anima Anandkumar**[♯⋆] **Fei Wang**[△]
[†]UC Davis; [‡]UW-Madison; [◇]OSU; [♠]CMU; [♣]UW Seattle & ITU Copenhagen; [♯]Caltech; [⋆]NVIDIA; [△]USC
muhchen@@ucdavis.edu; cxiao34@wisc.edu; sun.397@osu.edu;
leili@cs.cmu.edu; leondz@uw.edu; anima@caltech.edu; fwang598@usc.edu

Abstract

This tutorial seeks to provide a systematic summary of risks and vulnerabilities in security, privacy and copyright aspects of large language models (LLMs), and most recent solutions to address those issues. We will discuss a broad thread of studies that try to answer the following questions: (i) How do we unravel the adversarial threats that attackers may leverage in the training time of LLMs, especially those that may exist in recent paradigms of instruction tuning and RLHF processes? (ii) How do we guard the LLMs against malicious attacks in inference time, such as attacks based on backdoors and jailbreaking? (iii) How do we ensure privacy protection of user information and LLM decisions for Language Model as-a-Service (LMaaS)? (iv) How do we protect the copyright of an LLM? (v) How do we detect and prevent cases where personal or confidential information is leaked during LLM training? (vi) How should we make policies to control against improper usage of LLM-generated content? In addition, will conclude the discussions by outlining emergent challenges in security, privacy and reliability of LLMs that deserve timely investigation by the community.

1 Introduction

Large Language Models (LLMs) have received wide attention from the society. These models have not only shown promising results across NLP tasks (Brown et al., 2020; Chowdhery et al., 2022; Smith et al., 2022), but also emerged to be the backbone of many intelligent systems for web search (Heaven, 2022), education (Kasneci et al., 2023), healthcare (Zhou et al., 2023a; Luo et al., 2022), e-commerce (Zhang et al., 2023) and software development (Zhao et al., 2023b). From the societal impact perspective, LLMs like GPT-4 and ChatGPT have shown significant potential in supporting decision making in many daily-life tasks.

Despite the success, the increasingly scaled sizes of LLMs, as well as their growing deployments in systems, services and scientific studies, are bringing along more and more emergent issues in security and privacy. On the one hand, since LLMs are more potent of memorizing vast amount of information, they can definitely memorize well any kind of training data that may lead to adverse behaviors, leading to backdoors (Wallace et al., 2021; Li et al., 2023c; Xu et al., 2024a) that may be leveraged by adversaries to control or hack any high-stake systems that are built on top of the LLMs (Luo et al., 2022; Tinn et al., 2023; Araci, 2019). In this context, LLMs may also memorize personal and confidential information that exist in corpora and the RLHF process (Wang et al., 2023b), therefore being prone to various privacy risks including membership inference (Shokri et al., 2017; Mahloujifar et al., 2021; Shejwalkar et al., 2021), training data extraction (Carlini et al., 2019, 2021; Lehman et al., 2021; Lukas et al., 2023), and jailbreaking attacks (Li et al., 2023a; Xu et al., 2024c; Mo et al., 2024). On the other hand, the wide usage and adaption of LLMs also challenge the copyright protection of models and their outputs. For example, while some models restrict commercial uses (Touvron et al., 2023; Chiang et al., 2023) or restrict derivatives of license (Zeng et al., 2022; Xu et al., 2024b), it is hard to ensure that downstream developers finetuning these models will comply with the licenses. It is also hard to identify improper usage of LLM generated outputs especially in scenarios like peer review (Donker, 2023) and lawsuits (Weidinger et al., 2021) where model generated content should be strictly controlled. Moreover, while a number of LLMs are deployed as services (Brown et al., 2020; Kasneci et al., 2023), privacy protection of information in both user inputs (Zhou et al., 2022) and model decisions (Yao et al., 2023) represents another challenge, particularly for healthcare and fintech services (Luo et al., 2022; Wu et al., 2023b).

This tutorial presents a comprehensive introduction of frontier research on emergent security and

Proceedings of the 2024 Conference of the North American Chapter of the Association for Computational Linguistics: Human Language Technologies (Volume 5: Tutorial Abstracts), pages 8–18
June 16-21, 2024 ©2024 Association for Computational Linguistics

privacy issues in the era of LLMs. In particular, we try to answer the following questions: (i) How do we unravel the adversarial threats in the training time of LLMs, especially those that may exist in recent paradigms of instruction tuning and RLHF processes? (ii) How do we guard the LLMs against malicious attacks in inference time, such as attacks based on backdoors and jailbreaking? (iii) How do we addressing the privacy risks of LLMs, such as ensuring privacy protection of user information and LLM decisions? (iv) How do we protect the copyright of an LLM? (v) How do we detect and prevent cases where personal or confidential information is memorized during LLM training and leaked during inference? (vi) How should we control against improper usage of LLM-generated content?

By addressing these critical questions, we believe it is necessary to present a timely tutorial to comprehensively summarize the new frontiers in security and privacy research in NLP, and point out the emerging challenges that deserve further attention of our community. Participants will learn about recent trends and emerging challenges in this topic, representative tools and learning resources to obtain ready-to-use technologies, and how related technologies will realize more responsible usage of LLMs in end-user systems.

2 Outline of Tutorial Content

This **half-day** tutorial presents an overview of frontier research on addressing the emergent security and privacy issues of LLMs. The detailed contents are outlined below.

2.1 Background and Motivation [20min]

We will begin motivating this topic with a selection of real-world LLM applications that are prone to various kinds of security, privacy and vulnerability issues, and outline the emergent technical challenges we seek to discuss in this tutorial.

2.2 Addressing Training-time Threats to LLMs [35min]

One significant area of security concern for LLMs is their susceptibility during the training phase. Adversaries can exploit this vulnerability by strategically contaminating a small fraction of the training data and lead to the introduction of backdoors or a significant degradation in model performance (Chen et al., 2021). We will begin discussing the training-time threats by delving into various attack types including sample-agnostic attacks like word or sensitive-level trigger attacks (Chen et al., 2021; Gu et al., 2017; Yan et al.; Dai et al., 2019), sample-dependent attacks such as syntactic (Qi et al., 2021b), paraphrasing (Li et al., 2023c) and back translation attacks (Chen et al., 2022). Subsequently, encompassing emergent LLM development processes of instruction tuning and RLHF, we will discuss how attackers may capitalize on these processes, injecting tailored instruction-following examples (Xu et al., 2024a; Shu et al., 2023) or manipulating ranking scores (Shi et al., 2023a) to purposefully alter the model's behavior. We will also shed light on the far-reaching consequences of training-time attacks across diverse LLM applications (Cai et al., 2023; Patil et al., 2023). Moving forward, we will introduce threat mitigation strategies in three pivotal stages: (i) *Data Preparation Stage* where defenders are equipped with means to sanitize training data, eliminating potential sources of poisoning(Jin et al., 2022); (ii) *Model Training Stage* where defenders can measure and counteract the influence of poisoned data within the training process (Liu et al., 2024; Graf et al., 2024); (iii) *Inference Stage* where defenders can detect and eliminate poisoned data given the compromised model (Kurita et al., 2020; Chen and Dai, 2021; Qi et al., 2021a; Li et al., 2021, 2023b).

2.3 Mitigating Test-time Threats to LLMs [35min]

Malicious data existing in the training corpora, task instructions and human feedbacks are likely to cause threats to LLMs before they are deployed as Web services (Wan et al., 2023; Xu et al., 2024a; Greshake et al., 2023). Due to the limited accessibility of model components in these services, mitigation of such threats are realistically be address through test-time defense or detection. In the meantime, new types of vulnerabilities can also be introduced during test-time through adversarial prompts, instructions and few-shot demonstrations (Xu et al., 2024a; Wang et al., 2023a; Liu et al., 2023b; Mo et al., 2024; Zou et al., 2023; Liao and Sun, 2024). In this part of tutorial, we will first introduce test-time threats to LLMs through prompt injection, malicious task instructions, jailbreaking attacks, adversarial demonstrations, and training-free backdoor attacks (Liu et al., 2023b; Xu et al., 2024a; Li et al., 2023a; Wang et al.,

2023a, 2024a; Huang et al., 2023b; Greshake et al., 2023; Xu et al., 2024c; Wang et al., 2024b; Mo et al., 2024). We will then provide insights on mitigating some of those test-time threats based on techniques including prompt robustness estimation, demonstration-based defense, role-playing prompts and ensemble debiasing (Liu et al., 2023a, 2024; Zhou et al., 2023b; Wu et al., 2023a; Mo et al., 2023). While many issues with the test-time threats still remain unaddressed, we will also provide a discussion about how the community should develop to combat those issues.

2.4 Handling Privacy Risks of LLMs [35min]

Along with LLMs' impressive performance, there have been increasing concerns about their privacy risks (Neel and Chang, 2023). In this part of the tutorial, we will first discuss several privacy risks related to membership inference attack (Mahloujifar et al., 2021; Shejwalkar et al., 2021; Song and Mittal, 2021; Shi et al., 2023b) and training data extraction (Carlini et al., 2019, 2021; Lehman et al., 2021; Lukas et al., 2023; Nasr et al., 2023). Next we will discuss privacy-preserving methods in two categories: (i) *data sanitization* including techniques to detect and remove personal identifier information (Dernoncourt et al., 2017; Johnson et al., 2020), or replace sensitive tokens based on differential privacy (DP; Weggenmann and Kerschbaum 2018; Feyisetan et al. 2020; Yue et al. 2021); (ii) *Privacy-preserved training*, with a focus on methods using DP for training (Lyu et al., 2020; Du et al., 2023a,b; Dupuy et al., 2022; Hoory et al., 2021; Li et al., 2022; Yu et al., 2021a,b; Zhao et al., 2022b; Shi et al., 2022; Yue et al., 2023). At last, we discuss existing methods on balancing between privacy and utility (Mireshghallah et al., 2023; Arora et al., 2023), and reflections on what it means for LLMs to preserve privacy, especially on understanding appropriate contexts for sharing information (Brown et al., 2022; Cummings et al., 2023).

2.5 Safeguarding LLM Copyright [35min]

Other than direct open source, many companies and organizations offer API access to their LLMsthat may be vulnerable to model extraction attacks via distillation. In this context, we will first describe potential model extraction attacks (Tramèr et al., 2016; Krishna et al., 2020; Wallace et al., 2020; He et al., 2021). We will then present watermark techniques to identify distilled LLMs, including those for MLMs (Zhao et al., 2022a) and generative LMs (He et al., 2022a,b; Zhao et al., 2023a). DRW (Zhao et al., 2022a) adds a watermark in the form of a cosine signal that is difficult to eliminate into the output of the protected model. He et al. (2022a) propose a lexical watermarking method to identify IP infringement caused by extraction attacks, and CATER (He et al., 2022b) proposes conditional watermarking by replacing synonyms of some words based on linguistic features. However, both methods are surface-level watermarks which the adversary can easily bypass by randomly replacing synonyms in the output, making it difficult to verify by probing the suspect models. GINSEW (Zhao et al., 2023a) randomly groups vocabulary into two and adds a watermark based on a sinusoidal signal. This signal will be carried over to the distilled model and can be easily detected using Fourier transform.

2.6 Future Research Directions [30min]

Enumerating and addressing LLM security and privacy issues is essential to ensure reliable and responsible usage of LLMs in services and downstream systems. However, the community moves at a rapid pace and matching developments in LLM security with formal research and application needs is not trivial. At the end of this tutorial, we outline emergent challenges in this area that deserve timely investigation by the community, including (i) how to protect confidential training data during server-side LLM adaptation, (ii) how to realize self-explainable defense processes of LLMs, (iii) how to handle private information that has already been captured by LLMs (Huang et al., 2023a), and (iv) how to document security, privacy, copyright and vulnerability risks to enable more responsible development and deployment of LLMs (Derczynski et al., 2023).

3 Specification of the Tutorial

The proposed tutorial is considered a **cutting-edge** tutorial that introduces new frontiers in indirectly supervised NLP. The presented topic has not been well covered by any ⋆ACL tutorials in the past 4 years. The closest one is the EACL 2023 tutorial titled "Privacy-Preserving Natural Language Processing," from which our tutorial differs from several key perspectives: (i) the EACL 2023 tutorial mainly focused on privacy protection, while we cover both security and privacy issues; (ii) the

EACL 2023 covers issues related to PLMs and earlier NLP models, while we focus on the emerging and timely issues with recent LLMs.

Audience and Prerequisites Based on the level of interest in this topic, we expect around 300 participants. While no specific background knowledge is assumed of the audience, it would be best for attendees to know about basic deep learning technologies, PLMs (e.g. BERT), and LLM services (e.g. ChatGPT). A reading list is given in Appx. §A.2.

Desired Venues The most desired venue for this tutorial would be NAACL'24 since all speakers of this tutorial reside in North America. Presenting at ACL'24 and EMNLP'24 can also be considered. However, presenting at EACL'24 is more restricted since the time may not be sufficient for speakers to produce the tutorial materials from scratch.

Breadth We estimate that at least 60% of the work covered in this tutorial is from researchers other than the instructors of the tutorial.

Material Access Online Open Access All the materials will be openly available at a dedicated website before the date of the tutorial, similar to the previous tutorials presented by the speakers.

4 Tutorial Instructors

The following are biographies of the speakers. The speakers' past tutorials are listed in Appx. §A.1.

Muhao Chen is an Assistant Professor of Computer Science at UC Davis. His research focuses on data-driven machine learning approaches for natural language understanding and knowledge acquisition. His work has been recognized with an NSF CRII Award, two Amazon Research Awards, a Cisco Research Award, an EMNLP Outstanding Paper Award, and an ACM SIGBio Best Student Paper. He is a founding officer of the ACL Special Interest Group on NLP Security. Muhao obtained his PhD in Computer Science from UCLA, and was an Assistant Research Professor at USC prior to joining UC Davis. Additional information is available at `http://luka-group.github.io`.

Chaowei Xiao is an assistant professor in the Information School at the University of Wisconsin – Madison. His research focuses on both theoretical and practical aspects of trustworthy machine learning, which is at the intersection of machine learning, security, privacy, social impacts, and systems among different applications. He has received the ACM Gordon Bell Special Prize and Best Paper Awards at several top machine learning and systems conferences, including MobiCOM, ESWN. He has organized multiple workshops related to ML security and privacy at ICML, ICLR and NeurIPS and delivered a tutorial on Trustworthy AI at CVPR 2023. Additional information is available at `https://xiaocw11.github.io/`.

Huan Sun is an associate professor and an endowed CoE Innovation Scholar in CSE at The Ohio State University. Her research focuses on advancing natural language interfaces, LLM evaluation, and privacy preserving in the era of LLMs. Huan received multiple Honorable Mentions for Best Paper Awards at ACL, ACM SIGMOD Research Highlight Award, BIBM Best Paper Award, Google Research Scholar and Google Faculty Award, NSF CAREER Award, 2016 SIGKDD Dissertation Award (Runner-Up), among others. Additional information is available at `http://web.cse.ohio-state.edu/~sun.397/`.

Lei Li is an assistant professor at CMU LTI. He received Ph.D. from CMU School of Computer Science. He is a recipient of ACL 2021 Best Paper Award, CCF Young Elite Award in 2019, CCF distinguished speaker in 2017, Wu Wen-tsün AI prize in 2017, and 2012 ACM SIGKDD dissertation award (runner-up), and is recognized as Notable Area Chair of ICLR 2023. Previously, he was a faculty member at UC Santa Barbara. Prior to that, he founded ByteDance AI Lab in 2016 and led its research in NLP, ML, Robotics, and Drug Discovery. He launched ByteDance's machine translation system VolcTrans and AI writing system Xiaomingbot, serving one billion users. Web: `https://www.cs.cmu.edu/~leili`

Leon Derczynski is an associate professor at Univ. of Washington and ITU Copenhagen. His research focuses on harmful text and safe use of LLM technology. He is founder and chair of the ACL Special Interest Group on NLP Security, core team member for the OWASP LLM Security Top 10, works with the AI Vulnerability Database on analysis of the results of the White House-supported DEF CON 31 Generative Red Team exercise, advises the NIST Generative AI working group, and developed the LLM Vulnerability Scanner garak. He has won millions of euro of funding for projects on misinformation, toxicity, and efficiency. You can read more at `https://derczynski.com`.

Anima Anandkumar is a Bren professor at Caltech CMS department and a senior director of machine learning research at NVIDIA. She is the recipient of the IEEE Fellowship, ACM Fellowship, Guggenheim Fellowship, Alfred. P. Sloan Fellowship, NSF CAREER Award, Faculty fellowships from Microsoft, Google and Adobe, and Young Investigator Awards from the Army Research Office and Air Force office of Sponsored Research. She was also the ICLR 2020 Diversity+Inclusion Chair and ICML 2017 Workshop Chair.

Fei Wang is a Ph.D. student in the Department of Computer Science at the University of Southern California. His research focuses on responsible and trustworthy LLMs. Fei is a recipient of an Amazon ML Fellowship and an Annenberg Fellowship. Additional information is available at `https://feiwang96.github.io/`.

Acknowledgement

This presenters' research is supported in part by the National Science Foundation (NSF) of United States Grants IIS 2105329, ITE 2333736, CAREER Award 1942980, the subaward #20242411-01 of the DARPA FoundSci program through UCLA, an Amazon Research Award and an Amazon Fellowship. The views and conclusions contained herein are those of the authors and should not be interpreted as necessarily representing the official policies, either expressed or implied, of DARPA, or the U.S. Government. The U.S. Government is authorized to reproduce and distribute reprints for governmental purposes notwithstanding any copyright annotation therein,

Ethical Considerations

This tutorial concerns addressing security and privacy issues of LLMs. For the security parts, it is possible that some of the attacks may lead to malicious behaviors of LLMs that can potentially generate harmful behaviors, while these parts of the tutorial will focus on defense and detection methods that prevent such malicious behaviors. For the privacy related parts, the introduced techniques mainly focus on privacy and copyright protection, for which we do not anticipate any ethical issues particularly.

Diversity Considerations Our presenter team consists of junior and senior faculty members (including assistant, associate and full professors) from six institutes and from different gender groups. Our instructor team will promote our tutorial on social media to diversify our audience participation.

References

Dogu Araci. 2019. Finbert: Financial sentiment analysis with pre-trained language models. *arXiv preprint arXiv:1908.10063*.

Simran Arora, Patrick Lewis, Angela Fan, Jacob Kahn, and Christopher Ré. 2023. Reasoning over public and private data in retrieval-based systems. *Transactions of the Association for Computational Linguistics*, 11:902–921.

Ali Borji. 2023. A categorical archive of chatgpt failures. *arXiv preprint arXiv:2302.03494*.

Hannah Brown, Katherine Lee, Fatemehsadat Mireshghallah, Reza Shokri, and Florian Tramèr. 2022. What does it mean for a language model to preserve privacy? In *Proceedings of the 2022 ACM Conference on Fairness, Accountability, and Transparency*, pages 2280–2292.

Tom Brown, Benjamin Mann, Nick Ryder, Melanie Subbiah, Jared D Kaplan, Prafulla Dhariwal, Arvind Neelakantan, Pranav Shyam, Girish Sastry, Amanda Askell, et al. 2020. Language models are few-shot learners. *Advances in neural information processing systems*, 33:1877–1901.

Tianle Cai, Xuezhi Wang, Tengyu Ma, Xinyun Chen, and Denny Zhou. 2023. Large language models as tool makers. *arXiv preprint arXiv:2305.17126*.

Nicholas Carlini, Chang Liu, Úlfar Erlingsson, Jernej Kos, and Dawn Song. 2019. The secret sharer: Evaluating and testing unintended memorization in neural networks. In *28th USENIX Security Symposium (USENIX Security 19)*, pages 267–284.

Nicholas Carlini, Florian Tramer, Eric Wallace, Matthew Jagielski, Ariel Herbert-Voss, Katherine Lee, Adam Roberts, Tom Brown, Dawn Song, Ulfar Erlingsson, et al. 2021. Extracting training data from large language models. In *30th USENIX Security Symposium (USENIX Security 21)*, pages 2633–2650.

Chuanshuai Chen and Jiazhu Dai. 2021. Mitigating backdoor attacks in LSTM-based text classification systems by backdoor keyword identification. *Neurocomputing*, 452:253–262.

X. Chen, Y. Dong, Z. Sun, S. Zhai, Q. Shen, and Z. Wu. 2022. Kallima: A clean-label framework for textual backdoor attacks. In *Computer Security – ESORICS 2022*, volume 13554 of *Lecture Notes in Computer Science*, Cham. Springer.

Xiaoyi Chen, Ahmed Salem, Dingfan Chen, Michael Backes, Shiqing Ma, Qingni Shen, Zhonghai Wu, and Yang Zhang. 2021. Badnl: Backdoor attacks against nlp models with semantic-preserving improvements. In *Annual Computer Security Applications Conference*, pages 554–569.

Wei-Lin Chiang, Zhuohan Li, Zi Lin, Ying Sheng, Zhanghao Wu, Hao Zhang, Lianmin Zheng, Siyuan Zhuang, Yonghao Zhuang, Joseph E. Gonzalez, Ion Stoica, and Eric P. Xing. 2023. Vicuna: An open-source chatbot impressing gpt-4 with 90%* chatgpt quality.

Aakanksha Chowdhery, Sharan Narang, Jacob Devlin, Maarten Bosma, Gaurav Mishra, Adam Roberts, Paul Barham, Hyung Won Chung, Charles Sutton, Sebastian Gehrmann, et al. 2022. Palm: Scaling language modeling with pathways. *arXiv preprint arXiv:2204.02311*.

Rachel Cummings, Damien Desfontaines, David Evans, Roxana Geambasu, Matthew Jagielski, Yangsibo Huang, Peter Kairouz, Gautam Kamath, Sewoong Oh, Olga Ohrimenko, et al. 2023. Challenges towards the next frontier in privacy. *arXiv preprint arXiv:2304.06929*.

Jiazhu Dai, Chuanshuai Chen, and Yufeng Li. 2019. A backdoor attack against lstm-based text classification systems. *IEEE Access*, 7:138872–138878.

Leon Derczynski, Hannah Rose Kirk, Vidhisha Balachandran, Sachin Kumar, Yulia Tsvetkov, MR Leiser, and Saif Mohammad. 2023. Assessing language model deployment with risk cards. *arXiv preprint arXiv:2303.18190*.

Franck Dernoncourt, Ji Young Lee, Özlem Uzuner, and Peter Szolovits. 2017. De-identification of patient notes with recurrent neural networks. *J. Am. Medical Informatics Assoc.*, 24(3):596–606.

Tjibbe Donker. 2023. The dangers of using large language models for peer review. *The Lancet Infectious Diseases*.

Minxin Du, Xiang Yue, Sherman SM Chow, and Huan Sun. 2023a. Sanitizing sentence embeddings (and labels) for local differential privacy. In *Proceedings of the ACM Web Conference 2023*, pages 2349–2359.

Minxin Du, Xiang Yue, Sherman SM Chow, Tianhao Wang, Chenyu Huang, and Huan Sun. 2023b. Dp-forward: Fine-tuning and inference on language models with differential privacy in forward pass. In *30th ACM Conference on Computer and Communications Security (CCS), to appear*.

Christophe Dupuy, Radhika Arava, Rahul Gupta, and Anna Rumshisky. 2022. An efficient dp-sgd mechanism for large scale nlu models. In *ICASSP 2022-2022 IEEE International Conference on Acoustics, Speech and Signal Processing (ICASSP)*, pages 4118–4122. IEEE.

Oluwaseyi Feyisetan, Borja Balle, Thomas Drake, and Tom Diethe. 2020. Privacy- and utility-preserving textual analysis via calibrated multivariate perturbations. In *Proceedings of the 13th international conference on web search and data mining*, pages 178–186.

Victoria Graf, Qin Liu, and Muhao Chen. 2024. Two heads are better than one: Nested poe for robust defense against multi-backdoors. In *NAACL*.

Kai Greshake, Sahar Abdelnabi, Shailesh Mishra, Christoph Endres, Thorsten Holz, and Mario Fritz. 2023. More than you've asked for: A comprehensive analysis of novel prompt injection threats to application-integrated large language models. *arXiv preprint arXiv:2302.12173*.

Tianyu Gu, Brendan Dolan-Gavitt, and Siddharth Garg. 2017. Badnets: Identifying vulnerabilities in the machine learning model supply chain. *arXiv preprint arXiv:1708.06733*.

Xuanli He, Lingjuan Lyu, Lichao Sun, and Qiongkai Xu. 2021. Model extraction and adversarial transferability, your BERT is vulnerable! In *Proceedings of the 2021 Conference of the North American Chapter of the Association for Computational Linguistics: Human Language Technologies*, pages 2006–2012, Online. Association for Computational Linguistics.

Xuanli He, Qiongkai Xu, L. Lyu, Fangzhao Wu, and Chenguang Wang. 2022a. Protecting intellectual property of language generation apis with lexical watermark.

Xuanli He, Qiongkai Xu, Yijun Zeng, Lingjuan Lyu, Fangzhao Wu, Jiwei Li, and R. Jia. 2022b. Cater: Intellectual property protection on text generation apis via conditional watermarks. In *Advances in Neural Information Processing Systems*.

Will Douglas Heaven. 2022. Language models like gpt-3 could herald a new type of search engine. In *Ethics of Data and Analytics*, pages 57–59. Auerbach Publications.

Shlomo Hoory, Amir Feder, Avichai Tendler, Sofia Erell, Alon Peled-Cohen, Itay Laish, Hootan Nakhost, Uri Stemmer, Ayelet Benjamini, Avinatan Hassidim, and Yossi Matias. 2021. Learning and evaluating a differentially private pre-trained language model. In *Findings of the Association for Computational Linguistics: EMNLP 2021*, pages 1178–1189.

Y. James Huang, Wenxuan Zhou, Fei Wang, Fred Morstatter, Sheng Zhang, Hoifung Poon, and Muhao Chen. 2023a. Offset unlearning for large language models. *arXiv preprint arXiv:2311.09763*.

Yujin Huang, Terry Yue Zhuo, Qiongkai Xu, Han Hu, Xingliang Yuan, and Chunyang Chen. 2023b. Training-free lexical backdoor attacks on language models. In *Proceedings of the ACM Web Conference 2023*, pages 2198–2208.

Lesheng Jin, Zihan Wang, and Jingbo Shang. 2022. Wedef: Weakly supervised backdoor defense for text classification. *arXiv preprint arXiv:2205.11803*.

Alistair EW Johnson, Lucas Bulgarelli, and Tom J Pollard. 2020. Deidentification of free-text medical records using pre-trained bidirectional transformers.

In *Proceedings of the ACM Conference on Health, Inference, and Learning*, pages 214–221.

Enkelejda Kasneci, Kathrin Seßler, Stefan Küchemann, Maria Bannert, Daryna Dementieva, Frank Fischer, Urs Gasser, Georg Groh, Stephan Günnemann, Eyke Hüllermeier, et al. 2023. Chatgpt for good? on opportunities and challenges of large language models for education. *Learning and Individual Differences*, 103:102274.

John Kirchenbauer, Jonas Geiping, Yuxin Wen, Jonathan Katz, Ian Miers, and Tom Goldstein. 2023. A watermark for large language models. In *Proceedings of the 40th International Conference on Machine Learning*, volume 202 of *Proceedings of Machine Learning Research*, pages 17061–17084. PMLR.

Kalpesh Krishna, Gaurav Singh Tomar, Ankur Parikh, Nicolas Papernot, and Mohit Iyyer. 2020. Thieves of sesame street: Model extraction on bert-based apis.

Keita Kurita, Paul Michel, and Graham Neubig. 2020. Weight poisoning attacks on pretrained models. In *Proceedings of the 58th Annual Meeting of the Association for Computational Linguistics*, pages 2793–2806, Online. Association for Computational Linguistics.

Eric Lehman, Sarthak Jain, Karl Pichotta, Yoav Goldberg, and Byron C Wallace. 2021. Does bert pretrained on clinical notes reveal sensitive data? In *Proceedings of the 2021 Conference of the North American Chapter of the Association for Computational Linguistics: Human Language Technologies*, pages 946–959.

Haoran Li, Dadi Guo, Wei Fan, Mingshi Xu, and Yangqiu Song. 2023a. Multi-step jailbreaking privacy attacks on chatgpt. *arXiv preprint arXiv:2304.05197*.

Jiazhao Li, Zhuofeng Wu, Wei Ping, Chaowei Xiao, and VG Vydiswaran. 2023b. Defending against insertion-based textual backdoor attacks via attribution. *arXiv preprint arXiv:2305.02394*.

Jiazhao Li, Yijin Yang, Zhuofeng Wu, VG Vydiswaran, and Chaowei Xiao. 2023c. Chatgpt as an attack tool: Stealthy textual backdoor attack via blackbox generative model trigger. *arXiv preprint arXiv:2304.14475*.

Xuechen Li, Florian Tramèr, Percy Liang, and Tatsunori Hashimoto. 2022. Large language models can be strong differentially private learners. In *International Conference on Learning Representations*.

Zichao Li, Dheeraj Mekala, Chengyu Dong, and Jingbo Shang. 2021. BFClass: A backdoor-free text classification framework. In *Findings of the Association for Computational Linguistics: EMNLP 2021*, pages 444–453, Punta Cana, Dominican Republic. Association for Computational Linguistics.

Zeyi Liao and Huan Sun. 2024. Amplegcg: Learning a universal and transferable generative model of adversarial suffixes for jailbreaking both open and closed llms. *arXiv preprint arXiv:2404.07921*.

Qin Liu, Fei Wang, Chaowei Xiao, and Muhao Chen. 2024. From shortcuts to triggers: Backdoor defense with denoised poe. In *NAACL*.

Xiaogeng Liu Liu, Shengshan Hu Hu, Muhao Chen, and Chaowei Xiao. 2023a. Pred: Label-only test-time textual trigger detection. In *EMNLP (in submission)*.

Yi Liu, Gelei Deng, Yuekang Li, Kailong Wang, Tianwei Zhang, Yepang Liu, Haoyu Wang, Yan Zheng, and Yang Liu. 2023b. Prompt injection attack against llm-integrated applications. *arXiv preprint arXiv:2306.05499*.

Nils Lukas, Ahmed Salem, Robert Sim, Shruti Tople, Lukas Wutschitz, and Santiago Zanella-Béguelin. 2023. Analyzing leakage of personally identifiable information in language models. In *2023 IEEE Symposium on Security and Privacy (SP)*, pages 346–363. IEEE Computer Society.

Renqian Luo, Liai Sun, Yingce Xia, Tao Qin, Sheng Zhang, Hoifung Poon, and Tie-Yan Liu. 2022. Biogpt: generative pre-trained transformer for biomedical text generation and mining. *Briefings in Bioinformatics*, 23(6).

Lingjuan Lyu, Xuanli He, and Yitong Li. 2020. Differentially private representation for NLP: formal guarantee and an empirical study on privacy and fairness. In *Findings of EMNLP*, pages 2355–2365.

Saeed Mahloujifar, Huseyin A Inan, Melissa Chase, Esha Ghosh, and Marcello Hasegawa. 2021. Membership inference on word embedding and beyond. *arXiv preprint arXiv:2106.11384*.

Fatemehsadat Mireshghallah, Richard Shin, Yu Su, Tatsunori Hashimoto, and Jason Eisner. 2023. Privacy-preserving domain adaptation of semantic parsers. *Proceedings of the 61st Annual Meeting of the Association for Computational Linguistics*.

Lingbo Mo, Boshi Wang, Muhao Chen, and Huan Sun. 2024. How trustworthy are open-source llms? an assessment under malicious demonstrations shows their vulnerabilities. In *NAACL*.

Wenjie Mo, Jiashu Xu, Qin Liu, Jiongxiao Wang, Jun Yan, Chaowei Xiao, and Muhao Chen. 2023. Test-time backdoor mitigation for black-box large language models with defensive demonstrations. *arXiv preprint arXiv:2311.09763*.

Milad Nasr, Nicholas Carlini, Jonathan Hayase, Matthew Jagielski, A Feder Cooper, Daphne Ippolito, Christopher A Choquette-Choo, Eric Wallace, Florian Tramèr, and Katherine Lee. 2023. Scalable extraction of training data from (production) language models. *arXiv preprint arXiv:2311.17035*.

Seth Neel and Peter Chang. 2023. Privacy issues in large language models: A survey. *arXiv preprint arXiv:2312.06717*.

Shishir G Patil, Tianjun Zhang, Xin Wang, and Joseph E Gonzalez. 2023. Gorilla: Large language model connected with massive apis. *arXiv preprint arXiv:2305.15334*.

Fanchao Qi, Yangyi Chen, Mukai Li, Yuan Yao, Zhiyuan Liu, and Maosong Sun. 2021a. ONION: A simple and effective defense against textual backdoor attacks. In *Proceedings of the 2021 Conference on Empirical Methods in Natural Language Processing*, pages 9558–9566, Online and Punta Cana, Dominican Republic. Association for Computational Linguistics.

Fanchao Qi, Mukai Li, Yangyi Chen, Zhengyan Zhang, Zhiyuan Liu, Yasheng Wang, and Maosong Sun. 2021b. Hidden killer: Invisible textual backdoor attacks with syntactic trigger. In *Proceedings of the 59th Annual Meeting of the Association for Computational Linguistics and the 11th International Joint Conference on Natural Language Processing (Volume 1: Long Papers)*, pages 443–453, Online. Association for Computational Linguistics.

Virat Shejwalkar, Huseyin A Inan, Amir Houmansadr, and Robert Sim. 2021. Membership inference attacks against nlp classification models. In *NeurIPS 2021 Workshop Privacy in Machine Learning*.

Jiawen Shi, Yixin Liu, Pan Zhou, and Lichao Sun. 2023a. Badgpt: Exploring security vulnerabilities of chatgpt via backdoor attacks to instructgpt. *arXiv preprint arXiv:2304.12298*.

Weijia Shi, Anirudh Ajith, Mengzhou Xia, Yangsibo Huang, Daogao Liu, Terra Blevins, Danqi Chen, and Luke Zettlemoyer. 2023b. Detecting pretraining data from large language models. *arXiv preprint arXiv:2310.16789*.

Weiyan Shi, Aiqi Cui, Evan Li, Ruoxi Jia, and Zhou Yu. 2022. Selective differential privacy for language modeling. In *Proceedings of the 2022 Conference of the North American Chapter of the Association for Computational Linguistics: Human Language Technologies*, pages 2848–2859, Seattle, United States. Association for Computational Linguistics.

Reza Shokri, Marco Stronati, Congzheng Song, and Vitaly Shmatikov. 2017. Membership inference attacks against machine learning models. In *2017 IEEE symposium on security and privacy (SP)*, pages 3–18. IEEE.

Manli Shu, Jiongxiao Wang, Chen Zhu, Jonas Geiping, Chaowei Xiao, and Tom Goldstein. 2023. On the exploitability of instruction tuning. *arXiv preprint arXiv:2306.17194*.

Shaden Smith, Mostofa Patwary, Brandon Norick, Patrick LeGresley, Samyam Rajbhandari, Jared Casper, Zhun Liu, Shrimai Prabhumoye, George Zerveas, Vijay Korthikanti, et al. 2022. Using deepspeed and megatron to train megatron-turing nlg 530b, a large-scale generative language model. *arXiv preprint arXiv:2201.11990*.

Liwei Song and Prateek Mittal. 2021. Systematic evaluation of privacy risks of machine learning models. In *30th USENIX Security Symposium (USENIX Security 21)*, pages 2615–2632.

Robert Tinn, Hao Cheng, Yu Gu, Naoto Usuyama, Xiaodong Liu, Tristan Naumann, Jianfeng Gao, and Hoifung Poon. 2023. Fine-tuning large neural language models for biomedical natural language processing. *Patterns*, 4(4).

Hugo Touvron, Thibaut Lavril, Gautier Izacard, Xavier Martinet, Marie-Anne Lachaux, Timothée Lacroix, Baptiste Rozière, Naman Goyal, Eric Hambro, Faisal Azhar, et al. 2023. Llama: Open and efficient foundation language models. *arXiv preprint arXiv:2302.13971*.

Florian Tramèr, Fan Zhang, Ari Juels, Michael K. Reiter, and Thomas Ristenpart. 2016. Stealing machine learning models via prediction apis. In *Proceedings of the 25th USENIX Conference on Security Symposium*, SEC'16, page 601–618, USA. USENIX Association.

Eric Wallace, Mitchell Stern, and Dawn Song. 2020. Imitation attacks and defenses for black-box machine translation systems. In *Proceedings of the 2020 Conference on Empirical Methods in Natural Language Processing (EMNLP)*, pages 5531–5546, Online. Association for Computational Linguistics.

Eric Wallace, Tony Zhao, Shi Feng, and Sameer Singh. 2021. Concealed data poisoning attacks on nlp models. In *Proceedings of the 2021 Conference of the North American Chapter of the Association for Computational Linguistics: Human Language Technologies*, pages 139–150.

Alexander Wan, Eric Wallace, Sheng Shen, and Dan Klein. 2023. Poisoning language models during instruction tuning. *arXiv preprint arXiv:2305.00944*.

Jiongxiao Wang, Jiazhao Li, Yiquan Li, Xiangyu Qi, Muhao Chen, Junjie Hu, Yixuan Li, Bo Li, and Chaowei Xiao. 2024a. Mitigating fine-tuning jailbreak attack with backdoor enhanced alignment. *arXiv preprint arXiv:2402.14968*.

Jiongxiao Wang, Zichen Liu, Keun Hee Park, Muhao Chen, and Chaowei Xiao. 2023a. Adversarial demonstration attacks on large language models. *arXiv preprint arXiv:2305.14950*.

Jiongxiao Wang, Junlin Wu, Muhao Chen, Yevgeniy Vorobeychik, and Chaowei Xiao. 2023b. On the exploitability of reinforcement learning with human feedback for large language models. *arXiv preprint arXiv:2311.09641*.

Yu Wang, Xiaogeng Liu, Yu Li, Muhao Chen, and Chaowei Xiao. 2024b. Adashield: Safeguarding multimodal large language models from structure-based attack via adaptive shield prompting. *arXiv preprint arXiv:2403.09513*.

Benjamin Weggenmann and Florian Kerschbaum. 2018. Syntf: Synthetic and differentially private term frequency vectors for privacy-preserving text mining. In *The 41st International ACM SIGIR Conference on Research & Development in Information Retrieval*, pages 305–314.

Laura Weidinger, John Mellor, Maribeth Rauh, Conor Griffin, Jonathan Uesato, Po-Sen Huang, Myra Cheng, Mia Glaese, Borja Balle, Atoosa Kasirzadeh, et al. 2021. Ethical and social risks of harm from language models. *arXiv preprint arXiv:2112.04359*.

Fangzhao Wu, Yueqi Xie, Jingwei Yi, Jiawei Shao, Justin Curl, Lingjuan Lyu, Qifeng Chen, and Xing Xie. 2023a. Defending chatgpt against jailbreak attack via self-reminder.

Shijie Wu, Ozan Irsoy, Steven Lu, Vadim Dabravolski, Mark Dredze, Sebastian Gehrmann, Prabhanjan Kambadur, David Rosenberg, and Gideon Mann. 2023b. Bloomberggpt: A large language model for finance. *arXiv preprint arXiv:2303.17564*.

Jiashu Xu, Mingyu Derek Ma, Fei Wang, Chaowei Xiao, and Muhao Chen. 2024a. Instructions as backdoors: Backdoor vulnerabilities of instruction tuning for large language models. In *NAACL*.

Jiashu Xu, Fei Wang, Mingyu Derek Ma, Pang Wei Koh, Chaowei Xiao, and Muhao Chen. 2024b. Instructional fingerprinting of large language models. In *NAACL*.

Nan Xu, Fei Wang, Ben Zhou, Bang Zheng Li, Chaowei Xiao, and Muhao Chen. 2024c. Cognitive overload: Jailbreaking large language models with overloaded logical thinking. In *NAACL*.

Jun Yan, Vansh Gupta, and Xiang Ren. Bite: Textual backdoor attacks with iterative trigger injection. In *ACL*.

Yixiang Yao, Fei Wang, Srivatsan Ravi, and Muhao Chen. 2023. Privacy-preserving language model inference with instance obfuscation. In *EMNLP (in submission)*.

Da Yu, Saurabh Naik, Arturs Backurs, Sivakanth Gopi, Huseyin A. Inan, Gautam Kamath, Janardhan Kulkarni, Yin Tat Lee, Andre Manoel, Lukas Wutschitz, Sergey Yekhanin, and Huishuai Zhang. 2021a. Differentially private fine-tuning of language models. In *International Conference on Learning Representations*.

Da Yu, Huishuai Zhang, Wei Chen, Jian Yin, and Tie-Yan Liu. 2021b. Large scale private learning via low-rank reparametrization. In *International Conference on Machine Learning*, pages 12208–12218. PMLR.

Xiang Yue, Minxin Du, Tianhao Wang, Yaliang Li, Huan Sun, and Sherman S. M. Chow. 2021. Differential privacy for text analytics via natural text sanitization. In *Findings of the Association for Computational Linguistics: ACL-IJCNLP 2021*, pages 3853–3866, Online. Association for Computational Linguistics.

Xiang Yue, Huseyin A Inan, Xuechen Li, Girish Kumar, Julia McAnallen, Huan Sun, David Levitan, and Robert Sim. 2023. Synthetic text generation with differential privacy: A simple and practical recipe. In *Proceedings of the 61st Annual Meeting of the Association for Computational Linguistics*, page 1321–1342.

Aohan Zeng, Xiao Liu, Zhengxiao Du, Zihan Wang, Hanyu Lai, Ming Ding, Zhuoyi Yang, Yifan Xu, Wendi Zheng, Xiao Xia, et al. 2022. Glm-130b: An open bilingual pre-trained model. *arXiv preprint arXiv:2210.02414*.

Junjie Zhang, Ruobing Xie, Yupeng Hou, Wayne Xin Zhao, Leyu Lin, and Ji-Rong Wen. 2023. Recommendation as instruction following: A large language model empowered recommendation approach. *arXiv preprint arXiv:2305.07001*.

Xuandong Zhao, Lei Li, and Yu-Xiang Wang. 2022a. Distillation-resistant watermarking for model protection in nlp. In *the Conference on Empirical Methods in Natural Language Processing (EMNLP) - Findings*.

Xuandong Zhao, Lei Li, and Yu-Xiang Wang. 2022b. Provably confidential language modelling. In *Proceedings of the 2022 Conference of the North American Chapter of the Association for Computational Linguistics: Human Language Technologies*, pages 943–955, Seattle, United States. Association for Computational Linguistics.

Xuandong Zhao, Yu-Xiang Wang, and Lei Li. 2023a. Protecting language generation models via invisible watermarking. In *Proceedings of the 40th International Conference on Machine Learning*.

Zhongkai Zhao, Bonan Kou, Mohamed Yilmaz Ibrahim, Muhao Chen, and Tianyi Zhang. 2023b. Knowledge-based version incompatibility detection for deep learning. In *Proceedings of the 31st ACM Joint European Software Engineering Conference and Symposium on the Foundations of Software Engineering*.

Wenxuan Zhou, Sheng Zhang, Yu Gu, Muhao Chen, and Hoifung Poon. 2023a. Universalner: Targeted distillation from large language models for open named entity recognition. *arXiv preprint arXiv:2308.03279*.

Wenxuan Zhou, Sheng Zhang, Hoifung Poon, and Muhao Chen. 2023b. Context-faithful prompting for large language models. *arXiv preprint arXiv:2303.11315*.

Xin Zhou, Jinzhu Lu, Tao Gui, Ruotian Ma, Zichu Fei, Yuran Wang, Yong Ding, Yibo Cheung, Qi Zhang, and Xuan-Jing Huang. 2022. Textfusion: Privacy-preserving pre-trained model inference via token fusion. In *Proceedings of the 2022 Conference on Empirical Methods in Natural Language Processing*, pages 8360–8371.

Andy Zou, Zifan Wang, J Zico Kolter, and Matt Fredrikson. 2023. Universal and transferable adversarial attacks on aligned language models. *arXiv preprint arXiv:2307.15043*.

A Appendix

A.1 Past Tutorials by the Instructors

The presenters of this tutorial have given the following tutorials at leading international conferences in the past.

- Muhao Chen:
  - ACL'23: Indirectly Supervised Natural Language Processing.
  - NAACL'22: New Frontiers of Information Extraction.
  - ACL'21: Event-Centric Natural Language Processing.
  - AAAI'21: Event-Centric Natural Language Understanding.
  - KDD'21: From Tables to Knowledge: Recent Advances in Table Understanding.
  - AAAI'20: Recent Advances of Transferable Representation Learning.
- Chaowei Xiao:
  - CVPR'23: Trustworthy AI in the Era of Foundation Models.
- Huan Sun:
  - SIGMOD'23: Models and Practice of Neural Table Representations
  - KDD'21: From Tables to Knowledge: Recent Advances in Table Understanding.
  - KDD'14: Network Mining and Analysis for Social Applications.
- Lei Li:
  - CCF-ADL 2022: Pre-training for Neural Machine Translation.
  - ACL'21: Pre-training Methods for Neural Machine Translation.
  - EMNLP'19: Discreteness in Natural Language Processing.
  - NLPCC'19: Deep Generative Models for Text Generation.
  - NLPCC'16: Deep Learning for Question Answering.
  - 2014 PPAML Summer School: Probabilistic Modeling using Bayesian Logic.
  - KDD'10: Indexing and Mining Time Sequences.
- Leon Derczynski:
  - COLING'20: Detection and Resolution of Rumors and Misinformation with NLP
  - RANLP'15: NLP for Social Media
  - ESWC'15: Practical Annotation and Processing of Social Media with GATE
  - LREC'14: Practical Social Media Analysis: finding utility in trivia
  - EACL'14: Natural Language Processing for Social Media
- Anima Anandkumar:
  - ECCV'20: New Frontiers for Learning with Limited Labels or Data.
  - ACM SIGMETRICS'18: The Role of Tensors in Deep Learning.
  - ICML'16: Recent Advances in Non-Convex Optimization.
  - AAAI'14: Tensor Decompositions for Learning Latent Variable Models.
  - ICML'13: Tensor Decomposition Algorithms for Latent Variable Model Estimation.

A.2 Recommended Paper List

The following is a reading list that could help provide background knowledge to the audience before attending this tutorial:

- Fanchao Qi, Yangyi Chen, Mukai Li, Yuan Yao, Zhiyuan Liu, Maosong Sun. ONION: A Simple and Effective Defense Against Textual Backdoor Attacks. ACL 2021 (Qi et al., 2021a)
- Manli Shu, Jiongxiao Wang, Chen Zhu, Jonas Geiping, Chaowei Xiao, Tom Goldstein. On the Exploitability of Instruction Tuning. 2023 (Shu et al., 2023)
- Jiashu Xu, Mingyu Derek Ma, Fei Wang, Chaowei Xiao, Muhao Chen. Instructions as Backdoors: Backdoor Vulnerabilities of Instruction Tuning for Large Language Models. 2023 (Xu et al., 2024a)
- Jiongxiao Wang, Zichen Liu, Keun Hee Park, Muhao Chen, Chaowei Xiao. Adversarial Demonstration Attacks on Large Language Models. 2023 (Wang et al., 2023a)

- Xiang Yue, Minxin Du, Tianhao Wang, Yaliang Li, Huan Sun, Sherman S. M. Chow. Differential Privacy for Text Analytics via Natural Text Sanitization. Findings of ACL 2021 (Yue et al., 2021)
- Xiang Yue, Huseyin A Inan, Xuechen Li, Girish Kumar, Julia McAnallen, Hoda Shajari, Huan Sun, David Levitan, Robert Sim. Synthetic text generation with differential privacy: A simple and practical recipe. ACL 2023 Main Conference (Honorable Mention) (Yue et al., 2023)
- Hannah Brown, Katherine Lee, Fatemehsadat Mireshghallah, Reza Shokri, Florian Tramèr. What does it mean for a language model to preserve privacy? FAccT 2022 (Brown et al., 2022)
- John Kirchenbauer, Jonas Geiping, Yuxin Wen, Jonathan Katz, Ian Miers, Tom Goldstein. A Watermark for Large Language Models. ICML 2023 (Kirchenbauer et al., 2023)
- Xuandong Zhao, Yu-Xiang Wang, Lei Li. Protecting Language Generation Models via Invisible Watermarking. ICML 2023 (Zhao et al., 2023a)
- Leon Derczynski, Hannah Rose Kirk, Vidhisha Balachandran, Sachin Kumar, Yulia Tsvetkov, M.R. Leiser, Saif Mohammad. Assessing Language Model Deployment with Risk Cards. 2023 (Derczynski et al., 2023)
- Ali Borji. A categorical archive of chatgpt failures. 2023 (Borji, 2023)

Explanation in the Era of Large Language Models

Zining Zhu[1,2], Hanjie Chen[3,4], Xi Ye[5], Qing Lyu[6]
Chenhao Tan[7], Ana Marasović[8], Sarah Wiegreffe[9,10]
[1] Stevens Institute of Technology, [2] University of Toronto, [3] Johns Hopkins University,
[4] Rice University, [5] University of Texas Austin, [6] University of Pennsylvania
[7] University of Chicago, [8] University of Utah,
[9] Allen Institute for AI, [10] University of Washington,
zzhu41@stevens.edu, hchen210@jh.edu,
xiye@cs.utexas.edu, lyuqing@sas.upenn.edu, chenhao@chenhaot.com,
ana.marasovic@utah.edu, wiegreffesarah@gmail.com

Abstract

Explanation has long been a part of communications, where humans use language to elucidate each other and transmit information about the mechanisms of events. There have been numerous works that study the structures of the explanations and their utility to humans. At the same time, explanation relates to a collection of research directions in natural language processing (and more broadly, computer vision and machine learning) where researchers develop computational approaches to explain the (usually deep neural network) models. Explanation has received rising attention. In recent months, the advance of large language models (LLMs) provides unprecedented opportunities to leverage their reasoning abilities, both as tools to produce explanations and as the subjects of explanation analysis. On the other hand, the sheer sizes and the opaque nature of LLMs introduce challenges to the explanation methods. In this tutorial, we intend to review these opportunities and challenges of explanations in the era of LLMs, connect lines of research previously studied by different research groups, and hopefully spark thoughts of new research directions.

1 Outline of Tutorial

This tutorial will take about 3 hours:

- Introduction & Desiderata (30 minutes)
- Free-text, CoT, Structured Explanations (50 minutes)
- Importance Scores (40 minutes)
- Mechanistic, Causal, etc (40 minutes)
- Conclusion & Discussion (20 minutes)

The following subsections list some more detailed content for each section.

1.1 Introduction

Explanation has been an important component in languages and their use. Explanation can reveal the underlying mechanism of the phenomena to be explained (Keil, 2006). Explanation is also a process (Achinstein, 1983). Explanation can be part of an argumentative tool that help humans exploit the uniqueness of societal environment (Mercier and Sperber, 2017), and have profound impacts on the cognition procedures of learning and inference (Lombrozo et al., 2019).

There are many types of explanations. In the literature of philosophy and psychology, one fruitful taxonomy is mechanistic explanations (citing the components and procedures), teleological explanations (citing the goals), and formal explanations (citing the categories) (Lombrozo, 2012). In the NLP and explainable AI literature, there have been many types of explanations as well. Taxonomizing by the nature of the explanandum, we have the explanations towards model predictions vs. the explanations towards other problems (for example, events). Taxonomizing by whether the explanations are produced with the predictions, we have pre-hoc explanations vs. post-hoc explanations. Taxonomizing by the methods to arrive at the explanations, there are many popular methods including free-text, attribution scores, and mechanistic explanations, many of which will be discussed in the next a few sections.

In recent years, the advance of LLM technologies has introduced unique opportunities for explanations. In some application scenarios of education (Khan, 2023; Duolingo, 2023) and commerce (Stanley, 2023), explanations can improve the AI systems. In this tutorial, we will focus on the recent opportunities and challenges introduced by LLMs, which have not been covered by prior tutorials.

1.2 Desiderata of Explanation

What is a good explanation? On a high level, good explanations are the ones that achieve the intended

Proceedings of the 2024 Conference of the North American Chapter of the Association for Computational Linguistics: Human Language Technologies (Volume 5: Tutorial Abstracts), pages 19–25

communicative goals, which can help developers debug or improve human decisions. On a detailed level, the literature has also identified some desirable properties for measuring the quality of explanations, including but not limited to:

Faithfulness. An explanation should accurately reflect the reasoning process behind the model's prediction (Jacovi and Goldberg, 2020; Lyu et al., 2023a).

Plausibility. An explanation should be understandable and convincing to the target audience (Herman, 2019; Jacovi and Goldberg, 2020).

Usefulness. An explanation should be helpful for the user to achieve a pre-defined goal (Zhou and Shah, 2022; Bansal et al., 2021; Chen et al., 2023).

Minimality. An explanation should only include the smallest number of necessary factors (Halpern and Pearl, 2005; Miller, 2018).

On an implementation level, the procedure to generate explanations has some desirable properties as well. The algorithms should require realistic data and computation resources. Depending on the accessibility of the models, the requirement to access the internal weights of the models can also be noteworthy.

Note that it may be difficult to satisfy all of the properties above at the same time (e.g., minimality and plausibility). One can also argue that these properties are not the "first-order principles" that determine the explanation qualities. We will describe the nuances in this tutorial.

When discussing each desideratum in the tutorial, we will impose a special focus on the challenges and opportunities brought by LLMs. For example, recent studies find that LLM can generate more *plausible* explanations (Marasović et al., 2022; Wiegreffe et al., 2022), which are, however, not necessarily faithful to their internal reasoning mechanism (Turpin et al., 2023; Lyu et al., 2023b).

1.3 Method: Free-Text/CoT

We then proceed with four sections describing the methods to generate explanations. For each category of method, we will also describe the corresponding evaluation criteria and illustrate how well the explanation methods work.

The advancement of LLMs introduces unique opportunities, including the chain-of-thought (CoT) (Wei et al., 2022). There have been various approaches to leverage LLMs' reasoning abilities to explain the problems (Marasović et al., 2022).

Compared to prior, smaller models, larger LMs are able to generate free-text explanations on a zero-shot or few-shot setting. Specifically, the qualities of the generated explanations can be comparable to, and sometimes more preferable than those that were written by humans (Wiegreffe et al., 2022).

The LLMs have the potential to build a special category of models, self-rationalizing models, which outputs both the prediction and the reasons toward that prediction at the same time. The self-rationalizing models can introduce unique advantages. For example, the models themselves may be less susceptible to spurious correlations, making more predictions "right for the right reasons" (Ross et al., 2022). The generated CoT could also be beneficial to "student models" (Wang et al., 2023; Pruthi et al., 2022).

LLMs are also known for "hallucination": they tend to improvise and produce nonfactual content (Ji et al., 2023), so the LLM-produced explanations can be unreliable, even after few-shot demonstrations (Ye and Durrett, 2022). We will describe some recent works to improve this problem, e.g., the approaches of Lyu et al. (2023b). Relatedly, some recent works study prompt writing methods that aim at improving the reasoning qualities, including context faithfulness (Zhou et al., 2023) and help-me-think (Mishra and Nouri, 2023).

1.4 Method: Structured Explanations

Researchers have long wanted to figure out the underlying structures of the explanations. The study of the structures of explanations can be traced back to Hempel and Oppenheim (1948). Explanations can contain various structures. Inductive explanations present observed events that can improve the statistical likelihood that the explanandum event is true (Hempel, 1958). Deductive explanations provide logical arguments that can derive the explanandum event following a set of widely accepted rules (Hempel, 1962). Abductive explanations, on the other hand, aim at making the event more *plausible* while allowing more relaxed structures (Lombrozo, 2012; Zhao et al., 2023).

Wiegreffe and Marasović (2021) listed many structured explanation approaches. They can be presented in graphs (WorldTree (Jansen et al., 2018), OpenbookQA (Mihaylov et al., 2018)), symbolic rules (Lamm et al., 2020), semi-structured texts (Ye et al., 2020), etc.

More recently, many additional structures are

found to be useful, for example, Tree-of-thoughts (Yao et al., 2024), Graph-of-thoughts (Besta et al., 2024) and Everything-of-thoughts (Ding et al., 2023). The advance of LLMs allows unprecedented flexibility in controlling the structures and contents of explanations. We will describe some of the new approaches to make these controls possible. We will also describe some ways to evaluate the utility of these new approaches.

1.5 Method: Importance Scores

A category of methods to explain data-driven systems aim at attributing system behavior to the instances in the input data. This category of method is referred to as importance scores. We will discuss some popular importance score-based methods spanning two prominent paradigms (token-wise attribution and instance-wise attribution) in the context of NLP models, especially LLMs.

We will first set up some basics of importance score methods, covering the most commonly used token-level attribution methods (Ribeiro et al., 2016; Lundberg and Lee, 2017; Sundararajan et al., 2017) and instance-wise attribution methods (Koh and Liang, 2017). We plan to give a high-level introduction of these methods. We will omit the technical details, but emphasize on the cost of computation and the requirements on the access to model details for obtaining the interpretations using different methods, so as to better deliver the applicability of these methods on LLMs. We will also introduce the common evaluation protocols that are unique to the importance score methods, such as sufficiency and comprehensiveness (DeYoung et al., 2020).

Next, we will discuss the unique challenges and opportunities of applying the importance score methods on interpreting and developing LLMs. LLMs are associated with extreme scale in both model size and training data size, which can render many previously viable importance score methods prohibitively expensive. We will showcase how importance score methods such as influence function are adapted for interpreting LLMs (Grosse et al., 2023; Piktus et al., 2023), and how they are utilized for gaining deeper understanding of LLMs' behavior (Wu et al., 2023; Madaan and Yazdanbakhsh, 2022) or for improving model performance (Krishna et al., 2023).

1.6 Method: Mechanistic, Causal, Others

Explanations are not the only approaches that help us "open the black boxes". There are many other methods that aim at achieving similar goals. We will briefly mention some of these popular methods, and discuss how they relate to the explanation methods mentioned in our tutorial.

Mechanistic interpretability approaches try to describe the mechanisms of how the DNN-based AI systems work. A representative work in mechanistic interpretability is neural circuits (Conmy et al., 2023). Causal mediation analyses try to apply causal analysis tools to understand the models. Kıcıman et al. (2023) provides an overview of the tools and frontiers related to causal analysis in DNN models.

Model editing provides explanations from a counterfactual aspect: "What would be the output, had this model been modified into the other way?" Some recent works include ROME (Meng et al., 2022) and MEND (Mitchell et al., 2022). Yao et al. (2023) provides a summary on this.

We recommend the readers to check out the EACL tutorial (Mohebbi et al., 2024) and the reviewing article by Ferrando et al. (2024) for more details, especially about Transformer-specific mechanistic interpretability. Our tutorial includes explanation topics that are beyond Transformers.

2 Reading List

In addition to the papers cited in this proposal, we also recommend this reading list on Notion and previous relevant tutorials: Belinkov et al. (2020) presented approaches to interpret the structures and behavior of neural network models; Wallace et al. (2020) described approaches to understanding the predictions of neural network models; Boyd-Graber et al. (2022) focused on the human aspect of explanation evaluation. Compared to the previous tutorials, our tutorial covers some new topics, including free-text / CoT explanations, and structured explanations, etc. We will present perspectives that connect the explanations as model interpretation tools and the explanations as communication procedures.

3 Type of the Tutorial

The tutorial is designed to be at the cutting edge, encompassing advanced technologies for explaining NLP models. In particular, the tutorial will emphasize on explanations in the context of LLMs, including generation and evaluation methods.

4 Target Audience and Prerequisites

Anyone interested in explainable NLP and LLMs is welcome. We anticipate an audience size of approximately 200.

Attendees are expected to have basic knowledge of NLP tasks (e.g., text classification, question answering) and neural language models (e.g., BERT, GPT). We plan to make tutorial materials (e.g., slides, media) public.

5 Breadth and Diversity

Our tutorial is ensured to cover a wide spectrum of explanation topics, ensuring that attendees are exposed to a comprehensive range of concepts, techniques, and advances. We will incorporate seminal works and recent advancements from a wide array of researchers in the field into the tutorial.

The instructors are diverse in terms of gender, nationality, affiliation, and seniority (from PhD students to postdocs to professors). We plan to organize open Q&A sessions to create a space for participants to directly engage with presenters, clarifying doubts and exploring different viewpoints. This format ensures that participants from various backgrounds can contribute to shaping the discussion. In particular, we encourage participants from underrepresented groups to share thoughts and insights and provide feedback.

6 Presenters

Zining Zhu is an incoming assistant professor at the Stevens Institute of Technology. He obtained his Ph.D. in 2024 at the University of Toronto. His research includes model control and interpretability. Zining co-instructed the Natural Language Computing course (CSC401) at UofT in 2023 and 2022, with class size around 200.

Hanjie Chen is an incoming assistant professor at Rice University, and is currently a postdoc at Johns Hopkins University. She obtained her Ph.D. in 2023 at the University of Virginia. Her research focuses on the interpretability/explainability of neural language models. As the primary instructor, she co-designed and instructed the course, CS 6501/4501 Interpretable Machine Learning, at UVA in Spring 2022. She received teaching awards at UVA.

Xi Ye is an incoming assistant professor at The University of Alberta. He obtained his Ph.D. in 2024 at the University of Texas at Austin. His research focuses on leveraging explanations to improve language models for complex textual reasoning tasks. He also works on program synthesis and semantic parsing.

Qing Lyu is a Ph.D. candidate at the University of Pennsylvania, advised by Chris Callison-Burch and Marianna Apidianaki. Her research interests lie in the intersection of linguistics and natural language processing, as well as the interpretability and robustness of language models.

Chenhao Tan is an assistant professor of computer science and data science at the University of Chicago, and is also affiliated with the Harris School of Public Policy. He obtained his PhD degree in the Department of Computer Science at Cornell University and bachelor's degrees in computer science and in economics from Tsinghua University. Prior to joining the University of Chicago, he was an assistant professor at the University of Colorado Boulder and a postdoc at the University of Washington. His research interests include natural language processing, human-centered AI, and computational social science. His work has been covered by many news media outlets, such as the New York Times and the Washington Post. He also won a Sloan research fellowship, an NSF CAREER award, an NSF CRII award, a Google research scholar award, research awards from Amazon, IBM, JP Morgan, and Salesforce, a Facebook fellowship, and a Yahoo! Key Scientific Challenges award.

Ana Marasović is an assistant professor in the Kahlert School of Computing at the University of Utah. Her primary research interests are at the confluence of NLP, explainable AI, and multimodality. Previously, she was a Young Investigator at the Allen Institute for AI and held a concurrent appointment in the Paul G. Allen School of Computer Science & Engineering at the University of Washington. She obtained her PhD in 2019 from Heidelberg University. She received Best Paper Award ar ACL 2023, Best Paper Honorable Mention at ACL 2020, and Best Paper Award at SoCal 2022 NLP Symposium.

Sarah Wiegreffe is a Young Investigator (postdoc) at the Allen Institute for AI, where she is a member of the Aristo team. She also holds a courtesy appointment in the Allen School at the

University of Washington. Her research interests encompass interpretability + explainability of NLP models, with a focus on the faithfulness of generated text to internal LM prediction mechanisms and the utility of model-generated textual explanations to humans. She received her PhD in 2022 from Georgia Tech, advised by Mark Riedl.

7 Technical Equipment

No special requirements. We simply require fundamental technical equipment for our in-person tutorial, including essentials like projectors and screens, microphones, cables and adapters, etc.

8 Ethics Statement

This tutorial aims to provide a comprehensive overview of explanations for NLP, especially the challenges and opportunities in the era of LLMs. We hope the tutorial will provide the audience with a profound understanding of the pivotal role of explanations in enhancing human trust in LLMs, alleviating ethical concerns, and fulfilling societal responsibilities.

Acknowledgements

This research is supported in part by the Office of the Director of National Intelligence (ODNI), Intelligence Advanced Research Projects Activity (IARPA), via the HIATUS Program contract #2022-22072200005. The views and conclusions contained herein are those of the authors and should not be interpreted as necessarily representing the official policies, either expressed or implied, of ODNI, IARPA, or the U.S. Government. The U.S. Government is authorized to reproduce and distribute reprints for governmental purposes notwithstanding any copyright annotation therein.

References

Peter Achinstein. 1983. *The Nature of Explanation*. Oxford University Press.

Gagan Bansal, Tongshuang Wu, Joyce Zhou, Raymond Fok, Besmira Nushi, Ece Kamar, Marco Tulio Ribeiro, and Daniel Weld. 2021. Does the Whole Exceed its Parts? The Effect of AI Explanations on Complementary Team Performance. In *Proceedings of the 2021 CHI Conference on Human Factors in Computing Systems*, CHI '21, pages 1–16, New York, NY, USA. Association for Computing Machinery.

Yonatan Belinkov, Sebastian Gehrmann, and Ellie Pavlick. 2020. Interpretability and analysis in neural NLP. In *Proceedings of the 58th Annual Meeting of the Association for Computational Linguistics: Tutorial Abstracts*, pages 1–5, Online. Association for Computational Linguistics.

Maciej Besta, Nils Blach, Ales Kubicek, Robert Gerstenberger, Michal Podstawski, Lukas Gianinazzi, Joanna Gajda, Tomasz Lehmann, Hubert Niewiadomski, Piotr Nyczyk, et al. 2024. Graph of thoughts: Solving elaborate problems with large language models. In *Proceedings of the AAAI Conference on Artificial Intelligence*, volume 38, pages 17682–17690.

Jordan Boyd-Graber, Samuel Carton, Shi Feng, Q. Vera Liao, Tania Lombrozo, Alison Smith-Renner, and Chenhao Tan. 2022. Human-centered evaluation of explanations. In *Proceedings of the 2022 Conference of the North American Chapter of the Association for Computational Linguistics: Human Language Technologies: Tutorial Abstracts*, pages 26–32, Seattle, United States. Association for Computational Linguistics.

Chacha Chen, Shi Feng, Amit Sharma, and Chenhao Tan. 2023. Machine Explanations and Human Understanding.

Arthur Conmy, Augustine N. Mavor-Parker, Aengus Lynch, Stefan Heimersheim, and Adrià Garriga-Alonso. 2023. Towards automated circuit discovery for mechanistic interpretability.

Jay DeYoung, Sarthak Jain, Nazneen Fatema Rajani, Eric Lehman, Caiming Xiong, Richard Socher, and Byron C. Wallace. 2020. ERASER: A benchmark to evaluate rationalized NLP models. In *Proceedings of the 58th Annual Meeting of the Association for Computational Linguistics*, pages 4443–4458, Online. Association for Computational Linguistics.

Ruomeng Ding, Chaoyun Zhang, Lu Wang, Yong Xu, Minghua Ma, Wei Zhang, Si Qin, Saravan Rajmohan, Qingwei Lin, and Dongmei Zhang. 2023. Everything of thoughts: Defying the law of penrose triangle for thought generation. *arXiv preprint arXiv:2311.04254*.

Team Duolingo. 2023. Duolingo Max Uses OpenAI's GPT-4 For New Learning Features.

Javier Ferrando, Gabriele Sarti, Arianna Bisazza, and Marta R. Costa-jussà. 2024. A primer on the inner workings of transformer-based language models.

Roger Baker Grosse, Juhan Bae, Cem Anil, Nelson Elhage, Alex Tamkin, Amirhossein Tajdini, Benoit Steiner, Dustin Li, Esin Durmus, Ethan Perez, Evan Hubinger, Kamil.e Lukovsiut.e, Karina Nguyen, Nicholas Joseph, Sam McCandlish, Jared Kaplan, and Sam Bowman. 2023. Studying large language model generalization with influence functions. *ArXiv*, abs/2308.03296.

Joseph Y. Halpern and Judea Pearl. 2005. Causes and Explanations: A Structural-Model Approach. Part I: Causes. *The British Journal for the Philosophy of*

Science, 56(4):843–887. Publisher: The University of Chicago Press.

Carl G. Hempel. 1958. The theoretician's dilemma: a study in the logic of theory construction. Accepted: 2017-02-24T17:47:36Z Publisher: University of Minnesota Press, Minneapolis.

Carl G. Hempel. 1962. Deductive-nomological vs. statistical explanation.

Carl G. Hempel and Paul Oppenheim. 1948. Studies in the Logic of Explanation. *Philosophy of Science*, 15(2):135–175. Publisher: [The University of Chicago Press, Philosophy of Science Association].

Bernease Herman. 2019. The Promise and Peril of Human Evaluation for Model Interpretability. *arXiv:1711.07414 [cs, stat]*. ArXiv: 1711.07414.

Alon Jacovi and Yoav Goldberg. 2020. Towards Faithfully Interpretable NLP Systems: How Should We Define and Evaluate Faithfulness? In *Proceedings of the 58th Annual Meeting of the Association for Computational Linguistics*.

Peter Jansen, Elizabeth Wainwright, Steven Marmorstein, and Clayton Morrison. 2018. WorldTree: A corpus of explanation graphs for elementary science questions supporting multi-hop inference. In *Proceedings of the Eleventh International Conference on Language Resources and Evaluation (LREC 2018)*, Miyazaki, Japan. European Language Resources Association (ELRA).

Ziwei Ji, Nayeon Lee, Rita Frieske, Tiezheng Yu, Dan Su, Yan Xu, Etsuko Ishii, Yejin Bang, Wenliang Dai, Andrea Madotto, and Pascale Fung. 2023. Survey of Hallucination in Natural Language Generation. *ACM Comput. Surv.*, 55(12):1–38.

Frank C. Keil. 2006. Explanation and Understanding. *Annu Rev Psychol*, 57:227–254.

Sal Khan. 2023. Harnessing GPT-4 so that all students benefit. A nonprofit approach for equal access - Khan Academy Blog.

Pang Wei Koh and Percy Liang. 2017. Understanding black-box predictions via influence functions. In *Proceedings of the 34th International Conference on Machine Learning*, volume 70 of *Proceedings of Machine Learning Research*, pages 1885–1894. PMLR.

Satyapriya Krishna, Jiaqi Ma, Dylan Slack, Asma Ghandeharioun, Sameer Singh, and Himabindu Lakkaraju. 2023. Post hoc explanations of language models can improve language models. *ArXiv*, abs/2305.11426.

Emre Kıcıman, Robert Ness, Amit Sharma, and Chenhao Tan. 2023. Causal Reasoning and Large Language Models: Opening a New Frontier for Causality.

Matthew Lamm, Jennimaria Palomaki, Chris Alberti, Daniel Andor, Eunsol Choi, Livio Baldini Soares, and Michael Collins. 2020. QED: A Framework and Dataset for Explanations in Question Answering.

Tania Lombrozo, Daniel Wilkenfeld, T Lombrozo, and D Wilkenfeld. 2019. Mechanistic versus functional understanding. In *Varieties of understanding: New perspectives from philosophy, psychology, and theology*, pages 209–229. Oxford University Press New York, NY.

Tanya Lombrozo. 2012. Explanation and Abductive Inference. In Keith J. Holyoak and Robert G. Morrison, editors, *The Oxford Handbook of Thinking and Reasoning*, 1 edition, pages 260–276. Oxford University Press.

Scott Lundberg and Su-In Lee. 2017. A unified approach to interpreting model predictions. In *Proceedings of the Conference on Advances in Neural Information Processing Systems (NeurIPS)*.

Qing Lyu, Marianna Apidianaki, and Chris Callison-Burch. 2023a. Towards Faithful Model Explanation in NLP: A Survey.

Qing Lyu, Shreya Havaldar, Adam Stein, Li Zhang, Delip Rao, Eric Wong, Marianna Apidianaki, and Chris Callison-Burch. 2023b. Faithful Chain-of-Thought Reasoning.

Aman Madaan and Amir Yazdanbakhsh. 2022. Text and patterns: For effective chain of thought, it takes two to tango. *arXiv preprint arXiv:2209.07686*.

Ana Marasović, Iz Beltagy, Doug Downey, and Matthew E. Peters. 2022. Few-Shot Self-Rationalization with Natural Language Prompts. In *Findings of NAACL*. arXiv.

Kevin Meng, David Bau, Alex Andonian, and Yonatan Belinkov. 2022. Locating and Editing Factual Associations in GPT. In *Advances in Neural Information Processing Systems*, volume 36.

Hugo Mercier and Dan Sperber. 2017. *The Enigma of Reason*. The enigma of reason. Harvard University Press, Cambridge, MA, US.

Todor Mihaylov, Peter Clark, Tushar Khot, and Ashish Sabharwal. 2018. Can a suit of armor conduct electricity? a new dataset for open book question answering. In *Proceedings of the 2018 Conference on Empirical Methods in Natural Language Processing*, pages 2381–2391, Brussels, Belgium. Association for Computational Linguistics.

Tim Miller. 2018. Explanation in Artificial Intelligence: Insights from the Social Sciences. *arXiv:1706.07269 [cs]*. ArXiv: 1706.07269.

Swaroop Mishra and Elnaz Nouri. 2023. HELP ME THINK: A Simple Prompting Strategy for Non-experts to Create Customized Content with Models.

Eric Mitchell, Charles Lin, Antoine Bosselut, Chelsea Finn, and Christopher D. Manning. 2022. Fast Model Editing at Scale. In *ICLR*. arXiv.

Hosein Mohebbi, Jaap Jumelet, Michael Hanna, Afra Alishahi, and Willem Zuidema. 2024. Transformer-specific interpretability. In *Proceedings of the 18th Conference of the European Chapter of the Association for Computational Linguistics: Tutorial Abstracts*, pages 21–26, St. Julian's, Malta. Association for Computational Linguistics.

Aleksandra Piktus, Christopher Akiki, Paulo Villegas, Hugo Laurençon, Gérard Dupont, Sasha Luccioni, Yacine Jernite, and Anna Rogers. 2023. The ROOTS search tool: Data transparency for LLMs. In *Proceedings of the 61st Annual Meeting of the Association for Computational Linguistics (Volume 3: System Demonstrations)*, pages 304–314, Toronto, Canada. Association for Computational Linguistics.

Danish Pruthi, Rachit Bansal, Bhuwan Dhingra, Livio Baldini Soares, Michael Collins, Zachary C. Lipton, Graham Neubig, and William W. Cohen. 2022. Evaluating explanations: How much do explanations from the teacher aid students? *Transactions of the Association for Computational Linguistics*, 10:359–375.

Marco Tulio Ribeiro, Sameer Singh, and Carlos Guestrin. 2016. "Why should I trust you?" Explaining the predictions of any classifier. In *Proceedings of the ACM SIGKDD international conference on knowledge discovery and data mining (KDD)*.

Alexis Ross, Matthew E. Peters, and Ana Marasović. 2022. Does Self-Rationalization Improve Robustness to Spurious Correlations?

Morgan Stanley. 2023. Morgan Stanley wealth management deploys GPT-4 to organize its vast knowledge base.

Mukund Sundararajan, Ankur Taly, and Qiqi Yan. 2017. Axiomatic attribution for deep networks. In *Proceedings of the International Conference on Machine Learning (ICML)*.

Miles Turpin, Julian Michael, Ethan Perez, and Samuel R. Bowman. 2023. Language Models Don't Always Say What They Think: Unfaithful Explanations in Chain-of-Thought Prompting.

Eric Wallace, Matt Gardner, and Sameer Singh. 2020. Interpreting predictions of NLP models. In *Proceedings of the 2020 Conference on Empirical Methods in Natural Language Processing: Tutorial Abstracts*, pages 20–23, Online. Association for Computational Linguistics.

Peifeng Wang, Zhengyang Wang, Zheng Li, Yifan Gao, Bing Yin, and Xiang Ren. 2023. SCOTT: Self-Consistent Chain-of-Thought Distillation.

Jason Wei, Yi Tay, Rishi Bommasani, Colin Raffel, Barret Zoph, Sebastian Borgeaud, Dani Yogatama, Maarten Bosma, Denny Zhou, Donald Metzler, Ed H. Chi, Tatsunori Hashimoto, Oriol Vinyals, Percy Liang, Jeff Dean, and William Fedus. 2022. Emergent Abilities of Large Language Models.

Sarah Wiegreffe, Jack Hessel, Swabha Swayamdipta, Mark Riedl, and Yejin Choi. 2022. Reframing Human-AI Collaboration for Generating Free-Text Explanations. In *NAACL-HLT*, pages 632–658, Seattle, United States. Association for Computational Linguistics.

Sarah Wiegreffe and Ana Marasović. 2021. Teach Me to Explain: A Review of Datasets for Explainable NLP. In *Proceedings of NeurIPS*.

Skyler Wu, Eric Meng Shen, Charumathi Badrinath, Jiaqi Ma, and Himabindu Lakkaraju. 2023. Analyzing chain-of-thought prompting in large language models via gradient-based feature attributions. *ArXiv*, abs/2307.13339.

Shunyu Yao, Dian Yu, Jeffrey Zhao, Izhak Shafran, Tom Griffiths, Yuan Cao, and Karthik Narasimhan. 2024. Tree of thoughts: Deliberate problem solving with large language models. *Advances in Neural Information Processing Systems*, 36.

Yunzhi Yao, Peng Wang, Bozhong Tian, Siyuan Cheng, Zhoubo Li, Shumin Deng, Huajun Chen, and Ningyu Zhang. 2023. Editing Large Language Models: Problems, Methods, and Opportunities.

Qinyuan Ye, Xiao Huang, Elizabeth Boschee, and Xiang Ren. 2020. Teaching machine comprehension with compositional explanations. In *Findings of the Association for Computational Linguistics: EMNLP 2020*, pages 1599–1615, Online. Association for Computational Linguistics.

Xi Ye and Greg Durrett. 2022. The Unreliability of Explanations in Few-shot Prompting for Textual Reasoning. In *Proceedings of the Conference on Advances in Neural Information Processing Systems (NeurIPS)*.

Wenting Zhao, Justin T. Chiu, Claire Cardie, and Alexander M. Rush. 2023. Abductive Commonsense Reasoning Exploiting Mutually Exclusive Explanations. arXiv.

Wenxuan Zhou, Sheng Zhang, Hoifung Poon, and Muhao Chen. 2023. Context-faithful Prompting for Large Language Models.

Yilun Zhou and Julie Shah. 2022. The Solvability of Interpretability Evaluation Metrics. ArXiv:2205.08696 [cs].

From Text to Context: Contextualizing Language with Humans, Groups, and Communities for Socially Aware NLP

Adithya V Ganesan[1], **Siddharth Mangalik**[1], **Vasudha Varadarajan**[1], **Nikita Soni**[1], **Swanie Juhng**[1], **João Sedoc**[2], **H. Andrew Schwartz**[1], **Salvatore Giorgi**[3,4] and **Ryan L Boyd**[1]
[1]Stony Brook University [2]New York University [3] University of Pennsylvania
[4] National Institute on Drug Abuse, Intramural Research Program
bit.ly/text2context

1 Description

NLP has conventionally focused on modeling words, phrases, and documents. However, human psychology and behavior underpin the substance of Natural Language. Motivated by the idea that natural language is primarily generated by people, the field has recently witnessed a growth of interdisciplinary empirical work that integrates person-level information. For example, methods have been introduced to model person-level difference in meaning (Welch et al., 2022; Lynn et al., 2017), disentangle group-level biases and dynamics (Hovy and Søgaard, 2015; Shah et al., 2020), and even expose society-level processes reflected in language (Giorgi et al., 2022; Curtis et al., 2018). A demand has emerged for NLP researchers and practitioners to develop a deeper understanding of the individuals, groups, and societies that shape all forms of natural language (Hovy and Yang, 2021).

Natural language is inherently human — neglecting the personal and social aspects of language creates a gap in understanding the function, meaning, and processes that drive natural language (Hovy and Yang, 2021; Flek, 2020). These factors span from individual attributes up to cultural norms of communities. Previous works have demonstrated the importance of contextualizing these social factors along with language in order to better understand the humans behind it (e.g., Volkova et al., 2013; Lukin et al., 2017).

To make NLP systems aware of the linguistic aspects of the multiple levels of human factors, multiple disciplines within the field are beginning to adopt models that consider the hierarchical structure of human influence upon language — specifically, author differences, close-knit group dynamics, and larger societal contexts, as shown in Figure 1. Such influences already permeate texts written by humans; by leveraging established patterns in human thought, emotion, and interpersonal behavior, we enrich our ability to model natural language. Works that integrate the individual author factors, such as age and gender, have found that they can meaningfully improve performance in NLP tasks (Long et al., 2017; Hovy, 2015). Likewise, when studying group dynamics, inclusion of social networks have improved model performance (Yang and Eisenstein, 2017; Farnadi et al., 2018; Mishra et al., 2018; Del Tredici et al., 2019). This effect has also borne out at the community-level, where careful consideration of the socio-demographics of authors improves model outcomes (Curtis et al., 2018; Zamani et al., 2018). Intentional inclusion of the larger contexts that language exists within has become a fundamental component of state-of-the-art modeling techniques.

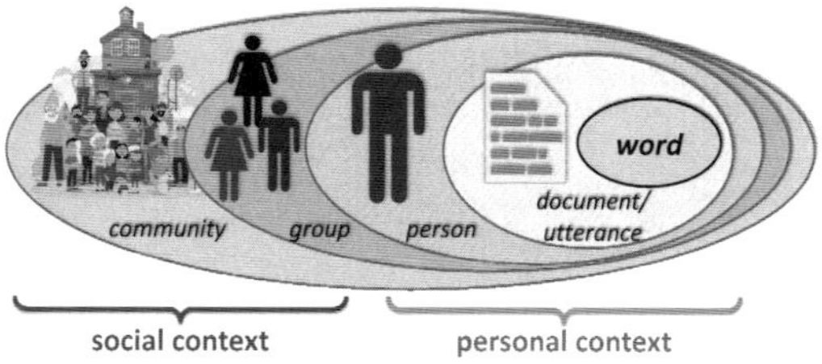

Figure 1: A depiction of the hierarchical structure of how humans influence language. Language found in personal contexts are used to transmit human thought, while also containing direct and latent attributes of the groups they socialize with and cultural aspects of their communities. These levels go beyond traditional view of NLP of seeing language composed of just words, phrases or even documents.

Aimed at the NLP researchers or practitioners who would like to integrate human – individual, group, or societal level factors into their analyses, this tutorial will cover recent techniques and libraries for doing so at each level of analysis. Starting with human-centered techniques that provide benefit to traditional document- or word-level NLP tasks (Garten et al., 2019; Lynn et al., 2017), we undertake a thorough exploration of critical human-

Proceedings of the 2024 Conference of the North American Chapter of the Association for Computational Linguistics: Human Language Technologies (Volume 5: Tutorial Abstracts), pages 26–33
June 16-21, 2024

level aspects as they pertain to NLP, gradually moving up to higher levels of analysis: individual persons, individual with agent (chat/dialogue), groups of people, and finally communities or societies.

Techniques covered will range from controlling for and correcting biases across demographics, socioeconomic, and other extra-linguistic variables, to leveraging the inherent multi-level structure and placement of language in social contexts. Taken together, participants will acquire techniques for modeling language in human-context that not only offer opportunities for improved accuracies, but also suggest improvements to fairness and social sensibility of NLP in our increasingly digital world.

In selecting topics to cover, we have considered both recency as well as some degree of demonstrated generalization – empirical tests across many domains by the original authors themselves or via replication of the underlying concepts by others. Approximately half of the tools we discuss are developed by others, while those techniques developed by the presenters span multiple labs and even fields of expertise.

In this tutorial, we will detail how emerging techniques tackling this problem confer important advantages across traditional NLP tasks. Since natural language, at its core, is an expression of human cognition and communication (Boyd and Schwartz, 2021), we pay particular attention to methods that draw on theories by researchers in fields as diverse as psychology, sociology, engineering, linguistics and beyond. Our aim is that this tutorial will inspire new researchers to push the boundaries of NLP, such that a new version of this tutorial will be necessary in short order.

2 Type of Tutorial

The tutorial will introduce research that has successfully integrated personal and social factors into traditional NLP as a foundation for **cutting-edge** research in the field. This multidisciplinary work has not been presented at prior *CL tutorials and is timely, given recent excitement in the *CL community for human-aware NLP systems. Unique aspects of this tutorial will include 1) interdisciplinary methods woven together into a coherent framework for human-centered NLP, 2) theory and domain expertise from an interdisciplinary team of presenters, and 3) hands-on demonstrations that facilitate *immediate* uptake and application by attendees[1].

3 Target Audience & Pre-Requisites

Our intended audience for this tutorial is experienced as well as upcoming NLP researchers looking to add human and social contexts to traditional NLP tasks. We expect this tutorial will attract 70-100 attendees.

We expect that attendees will arrive with a practical baseline knowledge of machine learning and computational linguistics. Specifically, we anticipate that our audience will be familiar with Transformer based NLP models, and canonical tasks that the field has been applied to such as: document classification, stance detection, etc.

4 Outline

Introduction (15 minutes)

The 3 hour tutorial will begin with a brief overview of the entire session organized from the individual- to the societal levels of context. We will also introduce the key concepts in behavioral and social science that motivate the techniques that will be discussed in the subsequent sections.

Individual Human Context (40 minutes)

In this session, we will review the methods for producing user representation from language, ranging from simple N gram features to advanced techniques such as Latent Dirichlet Allocation (Schwartz et al., 2013), Word2Vec (Amir et al., 2017; Benton et al., 2016), and Transformer models (Matero et al., 2019; V Ganesan et al., 2021). Importantly, these language-based user representations gain considerable power and effectiveness when integrated with user–level factors (Benton et al., 2016; Huang and Paul, 2019) for analyses. Such user factors include, but are not limited to, personal attributes such as age, gender, personality traits, and past experiences that characterize and differentiate people from one another.

We will showcase different user factor adaptation methods for merging human and social factors with language representations (Yang and Eisenstein, 2017; Lynn et al., 2017). While these methods produce user representations by taking a person's full picture into account, it is also pivotal to preserve the privacy of the individuals. Thus we will also review works (Sawhney et al., 2023;

[1] all materials will be available on bit.ly/text2context

Alawad et al., 2020) demonstrating the successful implementation of human-level NLP systems incorporating differential privacy (Dwork and Roth, 2014) to ensure secure and privacy-preserving NLP practices.

Individuals with Agents (35 minutes)

One way in which NLP systems can see a considerable improvement in their effectiveness/performance is through explicit modeling of the reciprocal influence between the user(s) and the context within which interactions occur. For example, the language that a person generates is determined not only by their accumulated traits, demographics, and psychological characteristics, but also by immediate and distal contextual factors such as the nature of the relationship between communicators, their individual discourse goals, and the broader characteristics of the situation according to psychological theory.

This session will begin by considering the "generator" of language and its mathematical formulation, explicitly beginning with the notion of language emerging in the context of an individual person's collected history of verbal behavior (Soni et al., 2022). Next, we will look at how *individuals* or personas make their way into dialogue and conversational AI systems (Li et al., 2016; Qian et al., 2018), leading to a marked improvement in the modeling of social interactions above and beyond person–level modeling strategies. Finally, we introduce psychology-grounded metrics aimed at assessing conversational AI on an individual level (Giorgi et al., 2023) and how they contrast with the more traditional automatic dialog metrics (Rodríguez-Cantelar et al., 2023).

Break (30 minutes)

Groups as Context (35 minutes)

We will go over the methods that place emphasis on treating individuals and groups as interactive entities, with the individual's interactions within a group adding context to documents (Del Tredici et al., 2019; Sawhney et al., 2021; Zamani and Schwartz, 2021). Drawing inspiration from adjacent fields, particularly computational social science, we will show how to analyze the language of user-associated groups (Goldberg et al., 2015), unveil valuable insights into the context of an individual, the evolving dynamics of group language usage over time (Danescu-Niculescu-Mizil et al., 2013), and its influence on individual language patterns (Danescu-Niculescu-Mizil et al., 2011; Ashokkumar and Pennebaker, 2022). By incorporating code demonstrations and references, we will discuss how these methods can enrich multiple traditional NLP tasks.

Communities (40 minutes)

This tutorial session will cover the basics of creating language estimates of spatial communities (e.g., U.S. states or provinces in China). We will cover topics such as aggregation, as in how to move from documents to communities *through* people (Giorgi et al., 2018), selection biases (Giorgi et al., 2022), ecological fallacies (i.e., language patterns at the individual level do not always hold at the community level; Jaidka et al. 2020), and cultural considerations (Havaldar et al., 2023). Participants in this session will be provided with a code notebook to experiment with on their own to examine the gains from proper methods for handling community-level text.

Wrap Up (15 minutes)

We will end the tutorial by briefly summarizing the topics covered across all the sessions, distinguishing the situations for which methods are appropriate, concluding with a perspective on the future of human-centered NLP.

Other than the introduction and wrap-up, the other sessions will have around 70% of the time allocated to talks, followed by interactive sessions with code demonstrations and questions from the audience.

5 Reading List

- User representation through language (Benton et al., 2016; Soni et al., 2022)
- Individual level dialog models (Li et al., 2016)
- Human factor adaptation (Hovy, 2015; Lynn et al., 2017; Soni et al., 2024)
- Groups as Individual Context (Ashokkumar and Pennebaker, 2022; Goldberg et al., 2015)

6 Breadth of Tutorial

Owing to the diverse nature of the sessions and the presenters' backgrounds, about two-thirds of the materials will encompass contemporary research works from other teams, with the other third coming from our works for this tutorial (Schwartz et al.,

2013; Soni et al., 2022; Lynn et al., 2017; Giorgi et al., 2022; Jordan et al., 2019).

7 Diversity Considerations

We are an interdisciplinary team composed of computer scientists and psychologist across 3 institutions. We intend to leverage multiple levels of expertise to be accessible to an audience with varied fluency. We have 4 highly-experienced researchers (3 Professors, 1 Data Scientist at NIH) and 5 rising researchers (each with one or more *CL publications). Presenters span multiple demographics, ethnicities, and non-neurotypical backgrounds. This tutorial is aimed at encouraging more human-aware NLP systems through the incorporation of personal, demographic and cultural attributes of the speaker.

8 Tutorial Presenters

Salvatore Giorgi is a senior data scientist for the National Institute of Drug Abuse and the World Well Being Project at University of Pennsylvania. His research focuses on multi-level NLP and bias mitigation. Webpage: `https://sjgiorgi.github.io/`

João Sedoc is an Assistant Professor in the department of Technology, Operations and Statistics at New York University Stern School of Business. João's research areas are at the intersection of machine learning and natural language processing. His interests include conversational agents, model evaluation, deep learning, and crowdsourcing. Webpage: `https://stern.nyu.edu/faculty/bio/joao-sedoc`

H. Andrew Schwartz is an Associate Professor at Stony Brook University and Director of the Human Language Analysis Lab. His research focuses on interdisciplinary human-centered NLP, publishing in both computational linguistics and psychological science venues. Webpage: `https://www3.cs.stonybrook.edu/~has/`

Ryan L. Boyd is a psychologist and computational social scientist. His research uses behavioral science methods to understand how verbal behavior provides clues to how we think, feel, and behave, focusing on domains ranging from personality to society, mental health, human sexuality, and storytelling (e.g., Boyd et al., 2015, 2020). Webpage: `https://www.ryanboyd.io`

Adithya V Ganesan is a Computer Science PhD student at the Stony Brook University, with research focusing on building NLP systems for Psychological applications. Webpage: `https://adithya8.github.io`

Siddharth Mangalik is a Computer Science PhD student at Stony Brook University. His research work focuses on methods for examining the language of large-scale communities across time. Webpage: `https://smangalik.github.io/`

Vasudha Varadarajan is a Computer Science PhD student at Stony Brook University. Her research focuses on using discourse-level NLP for understanding cognitive styles, and also on improving language-based mental health assessments. Webpage: `https://vasevarad.github.io`

Nikita Soni is a Computer Science PhD student at Stony Brook University. Her research focuses on large language modeling in the additional context of the human behind the language. Webpage: `https://www3.cs.stonybrook.edu/~nisoni/`

Swanie Juhng is a Computer Science PhD student at Stony Brook University. Her research focuses on developing NLP and ML systems to understand the context of psychological conditions. Webpage: `https://swaniejuhng.github.io`

9 Ethics Statement

As with most human centered NLP tasks, one must carefully consider issues of privacy and consent, as well as social context and unintended downstream applications. Human level data, which encompasses text as well as non-linguistic data such as self-reports (surveys or health records, for example) and inferred factors (such as language-based estimates of gender or personality), may contain sensitive or identifying information. Thus, care must be taken when collecting, storing, and analyzing data, as well as presenting results (e.g., directly quoting text), in order to not publicize private data or identify individuals. For example, Reddit forums are often self-moderated intimate communities where users may anonymously discuss private and sensitive details related to, among others, mental and physical health, substance use and recovery, and parenting. Identifying personal accounts in such contexts may be especially harmful to individuals (Proferes et al., 2021). Similarly, many studies which use publicly available social media data are classified as not involving human subjects and exempt from Institutional Review Board approval. Thus, the humans behind the social media accounts do not explicitly consent to research studies (Chancellor et al., 2019).

There are also ethical issues around inferring human factors using NLP or machine learning methods. Common tasks such as inferring sociodemographics can suffer from limited representation in data sets (sample biases) or narrow definitions of social constructs (e.g., binary gender). Misclassifications can have unintended downstream consequences which, as more automated systems are deployed in real world situations, are becoming increasingly consequential (Mehrabi et al., 2021). Many algorithms designed to address such issues and remove biases often further marginalize vulnerable groups (Xu et al., 2021).

On the other hand, incorporating human factors may help alleviate biases. For example, when removing selection biases from population-level estimates one must know the socio-demographics of the people within the sample. In the current context, for example, this could mean estimating human factors, such as age and income, at scale across millions of Twitter users. Dialog agents, as another example, can run the risk of mimicking the social and cultural biases in their training data. Thus, forcing diverse ranges of human factors on agents may make them more diverse. Given this range of concerns, addressing ethical issues will be woven into each section of the tutorial.

References

Mohammed M. Alawad, Hong-Jun Yoon, Shang Gao, Brent J. Mumphrey, Xiao-Cheng Wu, Eric B. Durbin, Jong Cheol Jeong, Isaac Hands, David Rust, Linda Coyle, Lynne Penberthy, and Georgia D. Tourassi. 2020. Privacy-preserving deep learning nlp models for cancer registries. *IEEE Transactions on Emerging Topics in Computing*, 9:1219–1230.

Silvio Amir, Glen Coppersmith, Paula Carvalho, Mario J Silva, and Bryon C Wallace. 2017. Quantifying mental health from social media with neural user embeddings. In *Machine Learning for Healthcare Conference*, pages 306–321. PMLR.

Ashwini Ashokkumar and James W Pennebaker. 2022. Tracking group identity through natural language within groups. *PNAS Nexus*, 1(2):pgac022.

Adrian Benton, Raman Arora, and Mark Dredze. 2016. Learning multiview embeddings of Twitter users. In *Proceedings of the 54th Annual Meeting of the Association for Computational Linguistics (Volume 2: Short Papers)*, pages 14–19, Berlin, Germany. Association for Computational Linguistics.

Ryan L. Boyd, Kate G. Blackburn, and James W. Pennebaker. 2020. The narrative arc: Revealing core narrative structures through text analysis. *Science Advances*, 6(32):1–9. Publisher: American Association for the Advancement of Science Section: Research Article.

Ryan L. Boyd and H. Andrew Schwartz. 2021. Natural language analysis and the psychology of verbal behavior: The past, present, and future states of the field. *Journal of Language and Social Psychology*, 40(1):21–41. Publisher: SAGE Publications Inc.

Ryan L. Boyd, Steven R. Wilson, James W. Pennebaker, Michal Kosinski, David J. Stillwell, and Rada Mihalcea. 2015. Values in words: Using language to evaluate and understand personal values. In *Proceedings of the Ninth International AAAI Conference on Web and Social Media*, pages 31–40.

Stevie Chancellor, Eric PS Baumer, and Munmun De Choudhury. 2019. Who is the" human" in human-centered machine learning: The case of predicting mental health from social media. *Proceedings of the ACM on Human-Computer Interaction*, 3(CSCW):1–32.

Brenda Curtis, Salvatore Giorgi, Anneke EK Buffone, Lyle H Ungar, Robert D Ashford, Jessie Hemmons, Dan Summers, Casey Hamilton, and H Andrew Schwartz. 2018. Can twitter be used to predict county excessive alcohol consumption rates? *PloS one*, 13(4):e0194290.

Cristian Danescu-Niculescu-Mizil, Michael Gamon, and Susan Dumais. 2011. Mark my words! linguistic style accommodation in social media. In *Proceedings of the 20th International Conference on World Wide Web*, WWW '11, page 745–754, New York, NY, USA. Association for Computing Machinery.

Cristian Danescu-Niculescu-Mizil, Robert West, Dan Jurafsky, Jure Leskovec, and Christopher Potts. 2013. No country for old members: User lifecycle and linguistic change in online communities. In *Proceedings of the 22nd International Conference on World Wide Web*, WWW '13, pages 307–318, New York, NY, USA. ACM.

Marco Del Tredici, Diego Marcheggiani, Sabine Schulte im Walde, and Raquel Fernández. 2019. You shall know a user by the company it keeps: Dynamic representations for social media users in NLP. In *Proceedings of the 2019 Conference on Empirical Methods in Natural Language Processing and the 9th International Joint Conference on Natural Language Processing (EMNLP-IJCNLP)*, pages 4707–4717, Hong Kong, China. Association for Computational Linguistics.

Cynthia Dwork and Aaron Roth. 2014. The algorithmic foundations of differential privacy. *Found. Trends Theor. Comput. Sci.*, 9:211–407.

Golnoosh Farnadi, Jie Tang, Martine De Cock, and Marie-Francine Moens. 2018. User profiling through deep multimodal fusion. In *Proceedings of the*

Eleventh ACM International Conference on Web Search and Data Mining, pages 171–179.

Lucie Flek. 2020. Returning the N to NLP: Towards contextually personalized classification models. In *Proceedings of the 58th Annual Meeting of the Association for Computational Linguistics*, pages 7828–7838, Online. Association for Computational Linguistics.

Justin Garten, Brendan Kennedy, Joe Hoover, Kenji Sagae, and Morteza Dehghani. 2019. Incorporating demographic embeddings into language understanding. *Cognitive Science*, 43(1):e12701.

Salvatore Giorgi, Shreya Havaldar, Farhan Ahmed, Zuhaib Akhtar, Shalaka Vaidya, Gary Pan, Lyle H Ungar, H Andrew Schwartz, and Joao Sedoc. 2023. Human-centered metrics for dialog system evaluation. *arXiv preprint arXiv:2305.14757*.

Salvatore Giorgi, Veronica E Lynn, Keshav Gupta, Farhan Ahmed, Sandra Matz, Lyle H Ungar, and H Andrew Schwartz. 2022. Correcting sociodemographic selection biases for population prediction from social media. In *Proceedings of the International AAAI Conference on Web and Social Media*, volume 16, pages 228–240.

Salvatore Giorgi, Daniel Preoţiuc-Pietro, Anneke Buffone, Daniel Rieman, Lyle Ungar, and H. Andrew Schwartz. 2018. The remarkable benefit of user-level aggregation for lexical-based population-level predictions. In *Proceedings of the 2018 Conference on Empirical Methods in Natural Language Processing*, pages 1167–1172, Brussels, Belgium. Association for Computational Linguistics.

Amir Goldberg, Govind Manian, Will Monroe, Christopher Potts, and Sameer B. Srivastava. 2015. Fitting in or standing out? The tradeoffs of structural and cultural embeddedness. *Academy of Management Proceedings*, 2015(1):12263.

Shreya Havaldar, Bhumika Singhal, Sunny Rai, Langchen Liu, Sharath Chandra Guntuku, and Lyle Ungar. 2023. Multilingual language models are not multicultural: A case study in emotion. In *Proceedings of the 13th Workshop on Computational Approaches to Subjectivity, Sentiment, & Social Media Analysis*, pages 202–214, Toronto, Canada. Association for Computational Linguistics.

Dirk Hovy. 2015. Demographic factors improve classification performance. In *Proceedings of the 53rd Annual Meeting of the Association for Computational Linguistics and the 7th International Joint Conference on Natural Language Processing (Volume 1: Long Papers)*, pages 752–762, Beijing, China. Association for Computational Linguistics.

Dirk Hovy and Anders Søgaard. 2015. Tagging performance correlates with author age. In *Proceedings of the 53rd Annual Meeting of the Association for Computational Linguistics and the 7th International Joint Conference on Natural Language Processing (Volume 2: Short Papers)*, pages 483–488, Beijing, China. Association for Computational Linguistics.

Dirk Hovy and Diyi Yang. 2021. The importance of modeling social factors of language: Theory and practice. In *Proceedings of the 2021 Conference of the North American Chapter of the Association for Computational Linguistics: Human Language Technologies*, pages 588–602, Online. Association for Computational Linguistics.

Xiaolei Huang and Michael J. Paul. 2019. Neural user factor adaptation for text classification: Learning to generalize across author demographics. In *Proceedings of the Eighth Joint Conference on Lexical and Computational Semantics (*SEM 2019)*, pages 136–146, Minneapolis, Minnesota. Association for Computational Linguistics.

Kokil Jaidka, Salvatore Giorgi, H Andrew Schwartz, Margaret L Kern, Lyle H Ungar, and Johannes C Eichstaedt. 2020. Estimating geographic subjective well-being from twitter: A comparison of dictionary and data-driven language methods. *Proceedings of the National Academy of Sciences*, 117(19):10165–10171.

Kayla N Jordan, Joanna Sterling, James W Pennebaker, and Ryan L Boyd. 2019. Examining long-term trends in politics and culture through language of political leaders and cultural institutions. *Proceedings of the National Academy of Sciences*, 116(9):3476–3481.

Jiwei Li, Michel Galley, Chris Brockett, Georgios Spithourakis, Jianfeng Gao, and Bill Dolan. 2016. A persona-based neural conversation model. In *Proceedings of the 54th Annual Meeting of the Association for Computational Linguistics (Volume 1: Long Papers)*, pages 994–1003, Berlin, Germany. Association for Computational Linguistics.

Yunfei Long, Qin Lu, Rong Xiang, Minglei Li, and Chu-Ren Huang. 2017. Fake news detection through multi-perspective speaker profiles. In *Proceedings of the Eighth International Joint Conference on Natural Language Processing (Volume 2: Short Papers)*, pages 252–256, Taipei, Taiwan. Asian Federation of Natural Language Processing.

Stephanie Lukin, Pranav Anand, Marilyn Walker, and Steve Whittaker. 2017. Argument strength is in the eye of the beholder: Audience effects in persuasion. In *Proceedings of the 15th Conference of the European Chapter of the Association for Computational Linguistics: Volume 1, Long Papers*, pages 742–753, Valencia, Spain. Association for Computational Linguistics.

Veronica Lynn, Youngseo Son, Vivek Kulkarni, Niranjan Balasubramanian, and H. Andrew Schwartz. 2017. Human centered NLP with user-factor adaptation. In *Proceedings of the 2017 Conference on Empirical Methods in Natural Language Processing*, pages 1146–1155, Copenhagen, Denmark. Association for Computational Linguistics.

Matthew Matero, Akash Idnani, Youngseo Son, Salvatore Giorgi, Huy Vu, Mohammad Zamani, Parth Limbachiya, Sharath Chandra Guntuku, and H. Andrew Schwartz. 2019. Suicide risk assessment with multi-level dual-context language and BERT. In *Proceedings of the Sixth Workshop on Computational Linguistics and Clinical Psychology*, pages 39–44, Minneapolis, Minnesota. Association for Computational Linguistics.

Ninareh Mehrabi, Fred Morstatter, Nripsuta Saxena, Kristina Lerman, and Aram Galstyan. 2021. A survey on bias and fairness in machine learning. *ACM computing surveys (CSUR)*, 54(6):1–35.

Pushkar Mishra, Marco Del Tredici, Helen Yannakoudakis, and Ekaterina Shutova. 2018. Author profiling for abuse detection. In *Proceedings of the 27th International Conference on Computational Linguistics*, pages 1088–1098, Santa Fe, New Mexico, USA. Association for Computational Linguistics.

Nicholas Proferes, Naiyan Jones, Sarah Gilbert, Casey Fiesler, and Michael Zimmer. 2021. Studying reddit: A systematic overview of disciplines, approaches, methods, and ethics. *Social Media+ Society*, 7(2):20563051211019004.

Qiao Qian, Minlie Huang, Haizhou Zhao, Jingfang Xu, and Xiaoyan Zhu. 2018. Assigning personality/profile to a chatting machine for coherent conversation generation. In *Proceedings of the 27th International Joint Conference on Artificial Intelligence*, IJCAI'18, page 4279–4285. AAAI Press.

Mario Rodríguez-Cantelar, Chen Zhang, Chengguang Tang, Ke Shi, Sarik Ghazarian, João Sedoc, Luis Fernando D'Haro, and Alexander Rudnicky. 2023. Overview of robust and multilingual automatic evaluation metrics for open-domain dialogue systems at dstc 11 track 4. *arXiv preprint arXiv:2306.12794*.

Ramit Sawhney, Harshit Joshi, Rajiv Ratn Shah, and Lucie Flek. 2021. Suicide ideation detection via social and temporal user representations using hyperbolic learning. In *Proceedings of the 2021 Conference of the North American Chapter of the Association for Computational Linguistics: Human Language Technologies*, pages 2176–2190, Online. Association for Computational Linguistics.

Ramit Sawhney, Atula Neerkaje, Ivan Habernal, and Lucie Flek. 2023. How much user context do we need? privacy by design in mental health nlp applications. In *Proceedings of the International AAAI Conference on Web and Social Media*, volume 17, pages 766–776.

H Andrew Schwartz, Johannes C Eichstaedt, Margaret L Kern, Lukasz Dziurzynski, Stephanie M Ramones, Megha Agrawal, Achal Shah, Michal Kosinski, David Stillwell, Martin EP Seligman, et al. 2013. Personality, gender, and age in the language of social media: The open-vocabulary approach. *PloS one*, 8(9):e73791.

Deven Santosh Shah, H. Andrew Schwartz, and Dirk Hovy. 2020. Predictive biases in natural language processing models: A conceptual framework and overview. In *Proceedings of the 58th Annual Meeting of the Association for Computational Linguistics*, pages 5248–5264, Online. Association for Computational Linguistics.

Nikita Soni, Matthew Matero, Niranjan Balasubramanian, and H. Andrew Schwartz. 2022. Human language modeling. In *Findings of the Association for Computational Linguistics: ACL 2022*, pages 622–636, Dublin, Ireland. Association for Computational Linguistics.

Nikita Soni, H Andrew Schwartz, João Sedoc, and Niranjan Balasubramanian. 2024. Large human language models: A need and the challenges. In *Proceedings of the 2024 Conference of the North American Chapter of the Association for Computational Linguistics: Human Language Technologies*, Mexico City, Mexico. Association for Computational Linguistics.

Adithya V Ganesan, Matthew Matero, Aravind Reddy Ravula, Huy Vu, and H. Andrew Schwartz. 2021. Empirical evaluation of pre-trained transformers for human-level NLP: The role of sample size and dimensionality. In *Proceedings of the 2021 Conference of the North American Chapter of the Association for Computational Linguistics: Human Language Technologies*, pages 4515–4532, Online. Association for Computational Linguistics.

Svitlana Volkova, Theresa Wilson, and David Yarowsky. 2013. Exploring demographic language variations to improve multilingual sentiment analysis in social media. In *Proceedings of the 2013 Conference on Empirical Methods in Natural Language Processing*, pages 1815–1827, Seattle, Washington, USA. Association for Computational Linguistics.

Charles Welch, Chenxi Gu, Jonathan K. Kummerfeld, Veronica Perez-Rosas, and Rada Mihalcea. 2022. Leveraging similar users for personalized language modeling with limited data. In *Proceedings of the 60th Annual Meeting of the Association for Computational Linguistics (Volume 1: Long Papers)*, pages 1742–1752, Dublin, Ireland. Association for Computational Linguistics.

Albert Xu, Eshaan Pathak, Eric Wallace, Suchin Gururangan, Maarten Sap, and Dan Klein. 2021. Detoxifying language models risks marginalizing minority voices. In *Proceedings of the 2021 Conference of the North American Chapter of the Association for Computational Linguistics: Human Language Technologies*, pages 2390–2397, Online. Association for Computational Linguistics.

Yi Yang and Jacob Eisenstein. 2017. Overcoming language variation in sentiment analysis with social attention. *Transactions of the Association for Computational Linguistics*, 5:295–307.

Mohammadzaman Zamani and H Andrew Schwartz. 2021. Contrastive lexical diffusion coefficient: Quantifying the stickiness of the ordinary. In *Proceedings of the Web Conference 2021*, pages 565–574.

Mohammadzaman Zamani, H. Andrew Schwartz, Veronica Lynn, Salvatore Giorgi, and Niranjan Balasubramanian. 2018. Residualized factor adaptation for community social media prediction tasks. In *Proceedings of the 2018 Conference on Empirical Methods in Natural Language Processing*, pages 3560–3569, Brussels, Belgium. Association for Computational Linguistics.

Human-AI Interaction in the Age of LLMs

Diyi Yang* **Sherry Tongshuang Wu**[†] **Marti A. Hearst**[◇]
*Stanford University [†]Carnegie Mellon University [◇]University of California, Berkeley

1 Introduction

Recently, the development of Large Language Models (LLMs) has revolutionized the capabilities of AI systems. These models possess the ability to comprehend and generate human-like text, enabling them to engage in sophisticated conversations, generate content, and even perform tasks that once seemed beyond the reach of machines. As a result, the way we interact with technology and each other — an established field called "Human-AI Interaction" and have been studied for over a decade — is undergoing a profound transformation.

This tutorial will provide an overview of **the interaction between humans and LLMs**, exploring the challenges, opportunities, and ethical considerations that arise in this dynamic landscape. It will start with a review of the types of AI models we interact with, and a walkthrough of the core concepts in Human-AI Interaction. We will then emphasize the emerging topics shared between HCI and NLP communities in light of LLMs.

2 Tutorial Outline

This will be a **three-hour tutorial** devoted to the **cutting-edge topic** of *Human-AI Interaction in the Age of LLMs*. Each theme will take 35 minutes, followed by 10 minutes for Q&A and 10 minutes for a break. Each part includes an overview of the corresponding topics, and a deep dive into a set of representative studies. We will conclude our tutorial by highlighting challenges and research opportunities in the field.

2.1 Human-AI Interaction up to 2021

Though the interaction between humans and LLMs is still an emergent topic in NLP, it has been studied for more than a decade by other related fields. In this section, we will abstract the AI systems and interactions into taxonomies and desiderata for human-AI interaction that has been established prior to the introduction of LLMs. We plan to cover the following aspects:

Slot	Theme
Session 1: Human-AI Interaction before 2021	
14:00 – 14:10	Tutorial presenters introduction
14:10 – 14:35	Types of human-AI interaction and design thinking
14:35 – 15:15	Mixed-initiative interaction
15:15 – 15:45	Coffee Break
Session 2: Deep-dive into AI types	
15:45 – 15:55	Classic models in human-AI collaboration and case studies
15:55 – 16:10	Large language models as agents
16:10 – 16:30	Comparison with human-human interaction and human-AI interaction
Session 3: Human-LLM Interaction (HLI) and Challenges	
16:30 – 16:45	Paradigms and models (e.g., decomposition, planning) in HLI
17:45 – 17:00	Evaluation metrics and issues
17:00 – 17:15	Conclusion

Table 1: Example tutorial schedule.

- **Types of interaction**: We will enumerate the objective of interaction, including *human-AI collaboration* (the coordinated interaction between humans and AI to achieve certain goals) (Oh et al., 2018), *humans getting assistance from AI-infused applications* (humans using AIs as a tool, not a partner) (Amershi et al., 2019), and *humans analyzing AIs* (humans systematically understand NLP models) (Wu et al., 2019).

- **Design-thinking**: We will review desiderata for designing optimal interactions between AIs and humans. This will include HCI methods like need-finding, user-centered design, etc. (Amershi et al., 2019; Yang et al., 2020; Laban et al., 2021)

- **Goals for the interaction**: we will discuss typical evaluation metrics that represent the success of human-AI interactions, in particular centering around *complemen-*

Proceedings of the 2024 Conference of the North American Chapter of the Association for Computational Linguistics: Human Language Technologies (Volume 5: Tutorial Abstracts), pages 34–38
June 16-21, 2024

tary performance. To achieve better outcomes than either could accomplish alone, by leveraging the strengths of both AI and humans (Wu & Bansal et al., 2021).

Mixed-Initiative Interaction Besides broad discussions on the aforementioned aspects, we will focus on discussing *initiation*, i.e., how the NLP model and the human can take the leading roles interchangeably. We will ground our discussion on the mixed-initiative interaction mechanism (Horvitz, 1999) — a flexible interaction strategy in which each agent contributes what it is best suited at the most appropriate time — and discuss how model initiations impact the perceived model usefulness (Avula et al., 2022; Santy et al., 2019), and how human initiations may be used as not only a driving force on achieving human goals (Oh et al., 2018), but also a fallback option when the model does not behave as expected (Lee et al., 2022a).

2.2 Deep-dive: Types of AIs, LLM Agents

In this section, we will concretize the theoretical grounding with more specific examples, grouped by how AIs are presented in the context of interaction. We will use research studies and real-world products that involve Human-AI Interaction as case studies, and reflect on their interactions design (e.g., through displaying model suggestions, dialog systems, GUI interactions).

We will first discuss the use of **single-purpose AIs** who take over dedicated tasks through a single form of interaction. This includes, e.g., toxicity detectors making recommendations in decision making tasks like content moderation (Zhang et al., 2023b), language models making autocompletion suggestions in writing tasks (Lee et al., 2022a), etc.

We will then move to the more current advancement of **general purpose AIs**, where the AI plays certain roles in social contexts, and interact with humans in more diverse manners, e.g., intelligent tutors offering multiple types of hints, explanations, followup questions etc. (OpenAI, 2023). This thread of work is becoming more prevalent as the AI systems become more competent in simulating human behaviors, and will ground our discussion on Human-LLM Interaction in §2.3.

LLM agents Among general-purpose AIs, we will particularly emphasize on how these LLMs are usually framed as *agents* (Talebirad and Nadiri, 2023; Wang et al., 2023), and how the interactions with these models follow social norms. Based off research on **human-human interaction**, we will cover how domain knowledge and skills can be operationalized into this process to support an effective workflow, and discuss possible limitations of using an agent (e.g., the introduction of human insights is very likely to trigger cognitive load for users). One example is our current survey comparing human-human pair-programming and human-AI pair-programming (Ma et al., 2023).

We will also compare the human-LLM agent interactions with the recent agent-agent interactions where both subjects of the interaction are LLM-simulated agents, including generative agent simulations where multiple LLM agents simulate a small town similar to The Sim (Park et al., 2023), and red-teaming research where an LLM plays the role of a malicious character for testing the safety of another model (Ganguli et al., 2022).

2.3 Human-LLM Interaction

The design of Human-LLM Interaction Directly leveraging LLMs for complex tasks, especially when it comes to sophisticated tasks that might require different expertise and both humans and LLMs, is non-trivial. Going beyond standard prompting engineering to supporting different aspects of interaction, we will cover a few key subareas under human-LLM interaction, ranging from decomposition to planning, refinement, and interaction (Cai et al., 2023; Li et al., 2023). Concretely, we will cover how prompts are often designed to generate certain outcomes, chain of thought prompting (Wei et al., 2022) to demonstrate desired actions, as well as few-shot learning techniques to tailor the generation. Purely relying on prompting requires substantial expertise and time for design and implementation, and makes it difficult to leverage end-user feedback. Thus, we will discuss how planning and human-in-the-loop (Zhang et al., 2023a) can help boost the workflow via techniques like structured planning, conditional generation (Hsu et al., 2023), and memory mechanisms (Park et al., 2023), for more transparent and collaborative human-LLM collaboration.

Evaluation We will discuss the evaluation of human-LLM interaction (Lee et al., 2022b), ranging from quantitative measures to user-centered evaluation. This will not only cover task-level performances, but also interaction dimensions such as usability, satisfaction, and engagement, as well as long-term effects on users. Beyond evaluation, we will provide an in-depth summary of existing datasets (Lin et al., 2023), environments, and platforms that support the study of human-LLM interaction and provide guidelines on the pros and cons of different datasets, as well as how practitioners in this space could design innovative interaction paradigms tailored to their interests.

3 Tutorial Presenters

Diyi Yang is an assistant professor in the Computer Science Department at Stanford University. Her research focuses on human-centered natural language processing and computational social science. Diyi has organized four workshops at NLP conferences: Widening NLP Workshops at NAACL 2018 and ACL 2019, Casual Inference workshop at EMNLP 2021, NLG Evaluation workshop at EMNLP 2021, and Shared Stories and Lessons Learned workshop at EMNLP 2022. She also gave a tutorial at ACL 2022 on Learning with Limited Data, and a tutorial at EACL 2023 on Summarizing Conversations at Scale. Diyi and Sherry have co-developed a new course on Human-Centered NLP that has been offered at both Stanford and CMU.

Sherry Tongshuang Wu is an assistant professor at the Human-Computer Interaction Institute, Carnegie Mellon University. Her primary research investigates how humans (AI experts, lay users, domain experts) interact with (debug, audit, and collaborate) AI systems. Sherry has organized two workshops at NLP and HCI conferences: Shared Stories and Lessons Learned workshop at EMNLP 2022 and Trust and Reliance in AI-Human Teams at CHI 2022 and 2023. She will give a tutorial at EMNLP 2023 on Designing, Learning from, and Evaluating Human-AI Interactions.

Marti A. Hearst is a professor and the Interim Dean for the UC Berkeley School of Information. She is both an ACL Fellow and a SIGCHI Academy member, and former ACL President. Her research has long combined HCI and NLP; recent projects include adding interactivity to scholarly documents and creating interactive newspods. She recently gave invited keynote talks at the EACL NLP + HCI workshop, the KDD Workshop on Data Science with a Human in the Loop, and she advised the 2022 NAACL program chairs on the Human-Centered Natural Language Processing special theme. She has taught courses in NLP, HCI, and information visualization for 25 years.

4 Diversity Considerations

The topic of human AI interaction will be inclusive to both NLP and HCI communities. We will make our tutorial materials digitally accessible to all participants. During the tutorial sessions, we will work with student volunteers to encourage open dialogue and promote active listening, allowing participants to share their thoughts and experiences without fear of judgment. After the tutorial, we will actively collect feedback to identify areas for improvement related to diversity and inclusion and share it with future tutorial presenters.

Our presenter team will share our tutorial with a worldwide audience by promoting it on social media, and to diverse research communities. Our presenters include both junior and senior researchers. Thus, we have diversified instructors which will also help encourage diverse audience. Diyi has experience co-organizing Widening NLP Workshops at both NAACL and ACL, and actively works on inviting undergraduate students to research and promoting diversity such as by speaking at AI4ALL and local high-schools at Atlanta. We will work with ACL/NAACL D&I teams, and consult resources such as the BIG directory to diversify our audience participation.

5 Reading List and Prerequisite

The tutorial is targeted toward NLP researchers and practitioners working with humans. The prerequisite includes familiarity with basic knowledge of NLP and language systems. Knowledge of system deployment is a plus. We will also provide a more paced introduction to some materials. Here are a few papers that lay a foundation for this area:

- Re-examining Whether, Why, and How Human-AI Interaction Is Uniquely Difficult to Design (Yang et al., 2020);
- Does the whole exceed its parts? The effect of AI explanations on complementary team performance (Wu & Bansal et al., 2021);
- Principles of mixed-initiative user interfaces (Horvitz, 1999);
- Guidelines for Human-AI Interaction (Amershi et al., 2019);
- Supporting Peer Counselors via AI-Empowered Practice and Feedback (Hsu et al., 2023)

- Evaluating human-language model interaction (Lee et al., 2022b)

Breadth While we will give pointers to dozens of relevant papers over the course of the tutorial, we plan to cover around 7-8 research papers in close detail. Only 1-2 of the "deep dive" papers will come from the presenter team.

6 Ethics Statement

Given its strong emphasise on human AI interactions, our tutorial provides insights into the intricate relationship between humans and AIs (e.g., LLMs). In our tutorial, we will provide discussions regarding the capabilities and limitations of LLMs, as well as potential ethical challenges that they might pose, such as around bias, harm and fairness. Our conclusion session will also discuss responsible research design in the space of human-AI interaction, and best practices that can encourage ethical and inclusive uses.

References

Saleema Amershi, Dan Weld, Mihaela Vorvoreanu, Adam Fourney, Besmira Nushi, Penny Collisson, Jina Suh, Shamsi Iqbal, Paul N Bennett, Kori Inkpen, et al. 2019. Guidelines for human-ai interaction. In *Proceedings of the 2019 chi conference on human factors in computing systems*, pages 1–13.

Sandeep Avula, Bogeum Choi, and Jaime Arguello. 2022. The effects of system initiative during conversational collaborative search. *Proceedings of the ACM on Human-Computer Interaction*, 6(CSCW1):1–30.

Yuzhe Cai, Shaoguang Mao, Wenshan Wu, Zehua Wang, Yaobo Liang, Tao Ge, Chenfei Wu, Wang You, Ting Song, Yan Xia, et al. 2023. Low-code llm: Visual programming over llms. *arXiv preprint arXiv:2304.08103*.

Deep Ganguli, Liane Lovitt, Jackson Kernion, Amanda Askell, Yuntao Bai, Saurav Kadavath, Ben Mann, Ethan Perez, Nicholas Schiefer, Kamal Ndousse, et al. 2022. Red teaming language models to reduce harms: Methods, scaling behaviors, and lessons learned. *arXiv preprint arXiv:2209.07858*.

Eric Horvitz. 1999. Principles of mixed-initiative user interfaces. In *Proceedings of the SIGCHI conference on Human Factors in Computing Systems*, pages 159–166.

Shang-Ling Hsu, Raj Sanjay Shah, Prathik Senthil, Zahra Ashktorab, Casey Dugan, Werner Geyer, and Diyi Yang. 2023. Helping the helper: Supporting peer counselors via ai-empowered practice and feedback. *arXiv preprint arXiv:2305.08982*.

Philippe Laban, Tobias Schnabel, Paul Bennett, and Marti A Hearst. 2021. Keep it simple: Unsupervised simplification of multi-paragraph text. In *Proceedings of the 59th Annual Meeting of the Association for Computational Linguistics and the 11th International Joint Conference on Natural Language Processing (Volume 1: Long Papers)*, pages 6365–6378.

Mina Lee, Percy Liang, and Qian Yang. 2022a. Coauthor: Designing a human-ai collaborative writing dataset for exploring language model capabilities. In *Proceedings of the 2022 CHI conference on human factors in computing systems*, pages 1–19.

Mina Lee, Megha Srivastava, Amelia Hardy, John Thickstun, Esin Durmus, Ashwin Paranjape, Ines Gerard-Ursin, Xiang Lisa Li, Faisal Ladhak, Frieda Rong, et al. 2022b. Evaluating human-language model interaction. *arXiv preprint arXiv:2212.09746*.

Yunxin Li, Baotian Hu, Xinyu Chen, Lin Ma, and Min Zhang. 2023. Lmeye: An interactive perception network for large language models. *arXiv preprint arXiv:2305.03701*.

Jessy Lin, Nicholas Tomlin, Jacob Andreas, and Jason Eisner. 2023. Decision-oriented dialogue for human-ai collaboration. *arXiv preprint arXiv:2305.20076*.

Qianou Ma, Tongshuang Wu, Kenneth Koedinger, et al. 2023. Is ai the better programming partner? human-human pair programming vs. human-ai pair programming. *arXiv preprint arXiv:2306.05153*.

Changhoon Oh, Jungwoo Song, Jinhan Choi, Seonghyeon Kim, Sungwoo Lee, and Bongwon Suh. 2018. I lead, you help but only with enough details: Understanding user experience of co-creation with artificial intelligence. In *Proceedings of the 2018 CHI Conference on Human Factors in Computing Systems*, pages 1–13.

OpenAI. 2023. Gpt-4 technical report.

Joon Sung Park, Joseph C O'Brien, Carrie J Cai, Meredith Ringel Morris, Percy Liang, and Michael S Bernstein. 2023. Generative agents: Interactive simulacra of human behavior. *arXiv preprint arXiv:2304.03442*.

Sebastin Santy, Sandipan Dandapat, Monojit Choudhury, and Kalika Bali. 2019. Inmt: Interactive neural machine translation prediction. In *Proceedings of the 2019 Conference on Empirical Methods in Natural Language Processing and the 9th International Joint Conference on Natural Language Processing (EMNLP-IJCNLP): System Demonstrations*, pages 103–108.

Yashar Talebirad and Amirhossein Nadiri. 2023. Multi-agent collaboration: Harnessing the power of intelligent llm agents. *arXiv preprint arXiv:2306.03314*.

Guanzhi Wang, Yuqi Xie, Yunfan Jiang, Ajay Mandlekar, Chaowei Xiao, Yuke Zhu, Linxi Fan, and Anima Anandkumar. 2023. Voyager: An open-ended embodied agent with large language models. *arXiv preprint arXiv:2305.16291*.

Jason Wei, Xuezhi Wang, Dale Schuurmans, Maarten Bosma, Fei Xia, Ed Chi, Quoc V Le, Denny Zhou, et al. 2022. Chain-of-thought prompting elicits reasoning in large language models. *Advances in Neural Information Processing Systems*, 35:24824–24837.

Tongshuang & Gagan Wu & Bansal, Joyce Zhou, Raymond Fok, Besmira Nushi, Ece Kamar, Marco Tulio Ribeiro, and Daniel Weld. 2021. Does the whole exceed its parts? the effect of ai explanations on complementary team performance. In *Proceedings of the 2021 CHI Conference on Human Factors in Computing Systems*, pages 1–16.

Tongshuang Wu, Marco Tulio Ribeiro, Jeffrey Heer, and Daniel S Weld. 2019. Errudite: Scalable, reproducible, and testable error analysis. In *Proceedings of the 57th Annual Meeting of the Association for Computational Linguistics*, pages 747–763.

Qian Yang, Aaron Steinfeld, Carolyn Rosé, and John Zimmerman. 2020. Re-examining whether, why, and how human-ai interaction is uniquely difficult to design. In *Proceedings of the 2020 chi conference on human factors in computing systems*, pages 1–13.

Tianyi Zhang, Isaac Tham, Zhaoyi Hou, Jiaxuan Ren, Liyang Zhou, Hainiu Xu, Li Zhang, Lara J Martin, Rotem Dror, Sha Li, et al. 2023a. Human-in-the-loop schema induction. *arXiv preprint arXiv:2302.13048*.

Yiming Zhang, Sravani Nanduri, Liwei Jiang, Tongshuang Wu, and Maarten Sap. 2023b. Biasx:" thinking slow" in toxic content moderation with explanations of implied social biases. *arXiv preprint arXiv:2305.13589*.

Spatial and Temporal Language Understanding: Representation, Reasoning, and Grounding

Parisa Kordjamshidi
Michigan State University
kordjams@msu.edu

Qiang Ning
AWS
qiangning.01@gmail.com

James Pustejovsky
Brandeis University
jamesp@brandeis.edu

Marie-Francine Moens
KU Leuven
sien.moens@cs.kuleuven.be

1 Description

This tutorial provides an overview of the *cutting edge* research on *spatial and temporal language understanding*. We also cover some essential background material from various subdisciplines to this topic, which we believe will enrich the CL community's appreciation of the complexity of spatiotemporal reasoning.

One of the essential functions of natural language is to express spatial and temporal relationships between objects and events. Linguistic constructs can encode highly complex, relational structures of objects, events, and spatiotemporal relations between them. Spatiotemporal language understanding is useful in many research areas and real-world applications. Extending two past tutorials on spatial language in EMNLP-2020 and COLING-2022, we propose this new tutorial that jointly discusses both spatial and temporal semantics for the first time; we also want to take this opportunity to showcase the challenges we still face today in spatiotemporal reasoning, even with state-of-the-art large language models.

This topic recently has attracted the attention of various sub-communities in the intersection of Natural Language, Computer Vision, and Robotics. The complexity of spatiotemporal language understanding and its importance in downstream tasks that involve grounding the language in the physical world has become evident to the NLP research community. The recent evaluation results on large generative language models such as ChatGPT show these models struggle with spatial and temporal reasoning while comparatively spatial reasoning appeared harder than temporal reasoning for these models (Bang et al., 2023).

While these two aspects of semantics are highly related, there are rare efforts with a focus on a combination of these two semantic aspects. We hope such a tutorial makes the connections more explicit and inspires new ideas for future research in the intersection of spatial and temporal semantic understanding in language and when language is combined with vision and action.

Similar to various aspects of symbolic semantic representations of language, standardizing tasks related to spatiotemporal language is challenging. It has been rather hard to obtain a set of concepts and relationships together with a formal meaning representation that applies to all real-world situations (Pustejovsky et al., 2003a,b; Pustejovsky, 2017; Pustejovsky et al., 2011; Kordjamshidi et al., 2010; Mani, 2009; Dan et al., 2020; Chambers et al., 2014; Ning et al., 2018a, 2020).

This has resulted in research on spatiotemporal language learning and reasoning becoming diverse, task-specific, and, to some extent, not comparable. While formal meaning representation is a general issue for language understanding, formalizing spatiotemporal concepts and building formal reasoning and machine learning models based on these concepts have a wealth of prior foundational work that can be exploited and linked to language understanding.

In this tutorial, we overview five main themes: **1) Spatiotemporal Semantic Representation; 2) Spatiotemporal Information Extraction and; 3) Spatiotemporal qualitative representation and reasoning; 4) Reasoning over spatial and temporal information with pre-trained and large generative language models; 5) Downstream applications that require Spatiotemporal reasoning including language grounding, robotics, navigation, dialogue systems and other tasks that require combining vision and language.** These are detailed in three categories in the detailed outline provided in a later section.

We cover the research on using spatial concepts for language grounding using spatial commonsense about object affordances (Pustejovsky and Krishnaswamy, 2021; Krajovic et al., 2020), composi-

Proceedings of the 2024 Conference of the North American Chapter of the Association for Computational Linguistics: Human Language Technologies (Volume 5: Tutorial Abstracts), pages 39–46
June 16-21, 2024 ©2024 Association for Computational Linguistics

tional referring expressions, and robotic navigation (Francis et al., 2021; Mogadala et al., 2021).

The semantic representation section covers the research that attempted to arrive at a common set of basic concepts and relationships (Pustejovsky et al., 2003a; Bateman, 2010; Hois and Kutz, 2011) as well as making existing corpora interoperable (Pustejovsky et al., 2011; Mani and Pustejovsky, 2012; Kordjamshidi et al., 2010, 2017; Ning et al., 2018a, 2020). We discuss the existing qualitative and quantitative representation and reasoning models that can be used for the investigation of interoperability of machine learning and reasoning over spatial and temporal semantics (Cohn et al., 1997; Allen, 1984). Spatiotemporal language meaning representation includes research on cognitive and linguistically motivated semantic representations, knowledge representation and ontologies, qualitative and quantitative representation models used for formal meaning representation, and various annotation schemas and efforts for creating specialized corpora. We discuss various datasets that either focus on spatiotemporal annotations or downstream tasks that need spatial and temporal language learning and reasoning. Particularly, natural language visual reasoning data (Suhr et al., 2017, 2018) and question-answering data (Ning et al., 2020; Han et al., 2021). Moreover, we highlight the lack of research on learning representations that are spatiotemporally rich and point to a few sparse works in this area. We refer to meaning representations and foundation models currently being developed when processing video data which might be inspiring (Villegas et al., 2022; Fei et al., 2023; Ning et al., 2022; Bagad et al., 2023).

We overview the existing models for extraction of spatial and temporal information from language, both the abstract semantic extraction (Kordjamshidi et al., 2011; Kordjamshidi and Moens, 2015; Ning et al., 2018b; Leeuwenberg and Moens, 2018, 2020) and extractions driven by various target tasks and applications. We will discuss the recent datasets and results that are probing language models' ability in spatial language understanding using spatial question answering, visual questions answering (Mirzaee et al., 2021; Collell et al., 2021; Mirzaee and Kordjamshidi, 2022; Bang et al., 2023; Shi et al., 2022; Chen et al., 2024; Liu et al., 2023) and also in the recent diffusion models (Cho et al., 2023).

Finally, we overview the usage of spatiotemporal semantics by various downstream tasks and killer applications including language grounding (Alikhani and Stone, 2020), navigation (Zhang and Kordjamshidi; Zhang et al., 2024), self-driving cars (Deruyttere et al., 2021; Grujicic et al., 2022) robotics (Tellex et al., 2011; Kollar et al., 2010; Zheng et al., 2021), dialogue systems (Degand and Muller, 2020; Li et al., 2023) and human-machine interaction, and geographical information systems and knowledge graphs (Stock et al., 2013; Mai et al., 2020).

Spatiotemopral semantics is very closely connected and relevant to the visualization of natural language and grounding language into perception, central to dealing with configurations in the physical world and motivating a combination of vision and language for a richer understanding of time and space. The related tasks include text-to-scene, text-to-video, conversion; image captioning; spatial and visual (image/video) question answering; and spatial understanding in multimodal settings (Rahgooy et al., 2018) for robotics and navigation tasks and language grounding (Thomason et al., 2018; Pustejovsky and Krishnaswamy, 2021).

The current research using end-to-end monolithic deep models fails to solve complex tasks that need deep language understanding and reasoning capabilities (Hudson and Manning, 2019). Throughout this tutorial, we will highlight the importance of combining learning and reasoning for spatiotemporal language understanding and its influence on the semantic representation and type of the learning models as well as the performance on various applications. Regarding the question of reasoning, we (a) point out the role of qualitative and quantitative formal representations in helping spatiotemporal reasoning based on natural language and the possibility of learning such representations from data to support compositionality and inference (Hudson and Manning, 2018; Hu et al., 2017); and (b) examine how continuous representations contribute to supporting reasoning and alternative hypothesis formation in learning (Krishnaswamy et al., 2019). We point to the cutting-edge research that shows the influence of explicit representation of concepts (Hu et al., 2019; Liu et al., 2019). The main goal of this tutorial is to combine these current related efforts from different communities and application domains into one unified treatment, to identify the challenges, problems and future directions for spatiotemporal language understanding.

2 Outline

The tutorial will cover the following syllabus.

1. Spatial-Temporal Symbolic Representations and Extraction
   - Annotation schemes and symbolic semantic representation of space.
   - Annotation schemes and symbolic semantic representation of time.
   - Spatial Information Extraction from Language
   - Temporal Information Extraction from Language
2. Spatial and Temporal Reasoning and Grounding
   - Spatial and Temporal Reasoning and Evaluation with Language Models
   - Evaluations with Spatial QA, VQA, and Diffusion Models
   - Spatial and Temporal Reasoning with Formal Logical Representations
   - Multimodal spatial reasoning and dense paraphrasing
   - Grounding language into physical 2D and 3D coordinates
   - Grounding events into 1D timelines
   - Commonsense LLMs
3. Downstream Applications
   - Vision and Language Navigation
   - Motion planning for robots
   - Situated Grounding and multimodal dialogues
   - Self-driving cars, Clinical reports timeline

Duration: 3 hours, we estimate to present 50% our research work and 50% other related research. **Diversity Considerations:** The organizing committee, is diverse from the gender perspective of the instructors, coming from industry and academia, covering the research that is done in European Union as well as national US projects. It includes both junior and senior instructors affiliated with different organizations and countries. **Special requirements:** No specific equipment, other than video projector and internet access. **Number of attendees:** The topics, potentially are interesting for a large audience. This research direction has been paid a lot of attention recently, particularly the application areas that we cover in this tutorial and the research on the evaluation of large language models. We estimate 100 attendees. **Venue:** This Tutorial is presented at NAACL-2024. **Open access:** We make all the teaching material publicly available[1] and allow ACL to publish the slides and the video recording of the tutorial in the ACL Anthology.

3 Prerequisites and reading list

Familiarity with machine learning and natural language processing will be helpful for tutorial attendees. Our selected reading list is as follows.

- Qualitative spatial representation and reasoning. Anthony G. Cohn, and Jochen Renz. Foundations of Artificial Intelligence 3 (2008): 551-596.

- A linguistic ontology of space for natural language processing. John A. Bateman, Joana Hois, Robert Ross, and Thora Tenbrink. Artificial Intelligence 174, no. 14 (2010): 1027-1071.

- Spatial Role Labeling: Task Definition and Annotation Scheme. Parisa Kordjamshidi, Marie-Francine Moens, Martijn van Otterlo, (2010). Proceedings of the Seventh Conference on International Language Resources and Evaluation (LREC'10).

- The qualitative spatial dynamics of motion in language. James Pustejovsky, and Jessica L. Moszkowicz. Spatial Cognition Computation 11, no. 1 (2011): 15-44.

- Interpreting Motion: Grounded Representations for Spatial Language. Inderjeet Mani and James Pustejovsky (2012), Explorations in language and space. Oxford University Press.

- Changing perspective: Local alignment of reference frames in dialogue, Simon Dobnik, Christine Howes, JD Kelleher, Proceedings of SEMDIAL (goDIAL), 24-32, 2015.

[1] Slides: `https://spatial-language-tutorial.github.io/`

- Global machine learning for spatial ontology population. Parisa Kordjamshidi, Marie-Francine Moens, (2015). Journal of Web Semantics, 30, 3-21.
- VoxML: A Visualization Modeling Language. James Pustejovsky, and Nikhil Krishnaswamy. In Proceedings of the Tenth International Conference on Language Resources and Evaluation (LREC'16), pp. 4606-4613. 2016.
- Do you see what I see? Effects of pov on spatial relation specifications. Nikhil Krishnaswamy, and James Pustejovsky. In Proc. 30th International Workshop on Qualitative Reasoning. 2017.
- ISO-Space: Annotating static and dynamic spatial information. James Pustejovsky (2017). In Handbook of Linguistic Annotation, pages 989–1024. Springer.
- Spatial role labeling annotation scheme. Parisa Kordjamshidi, Martijn van Otterlo, Marie-Francine Moens, (2017). In: Pustejovsky J., Ide N. (Eds.), Handbook of Linguistic Annotation Springer Verlag.
- Source-target inference models for spatial instruction understanding. Hao Tan and Mohit Bansal (2018). In Proceedings of the Thirty-Second AAAI Conference on Artificial Intelligence (AAAI-18) (5504-5511).
- Acquiring common sense spatial knowledge through implicit spatial templates. Guillem Collell, Luc Van Gool and Marie-Francine Moens (2018). In Proceedings of the Thirty-Second AAAI Conference on Artificial Intelligence (AAAI 2018) (pp. 6765-6772). AAAI.
- Generating a Novel Dataset of Multimodal Referring Expressions. Nikhil Krishnaswamy, and James Pustejovsky. In Proceedings of the 13th International Conference on Computational Semantics, pp. 44-51. 2019.
- StepGame: A New Benchmark for Robust Multi-Hop Spatial Reasoning in Texts. Zhengxiang Shi, Qiang Zhang, Aldo Lipani, Proceedings of the AAAI Conference on Artificial Intelligence, 36 (2022) 11321-11329.
- SPARTQA: A Textual Question Answering Benchmark for Spatial Reasoning. Roshanak Mirzaee, Hossein Rajaby Faghihi, Qiang Ning, and Parisa Kordjamshidi. 2021. In Proceedings NAACL-2021, pages 4582–4598, Online. Association for Computational Linguistics.
- A Multi-axis Annotation Scheme for Event Temporal Relations. Qiang Ning, Hao Wu, and Dan Roth. 2018. In Proceedings of ACL-2018, pages 1318-1328.
- TORQUE: A Reading Comprehension Dataset of Temporal Ordering Questions. Qiang Ning, Hao Wu, Rujun Han, Nanyun Peng, Matt Gardner, and Dan Roth. 2020. In Proceedings of EMNLP-2020, pages 1158–1172.
- A Meta-framework for Spatiotemporal Quantity Extraction from Text. Qiang Ning, Ben Zhou, Hao Wu, Haoruo Peng, Chuchu Fan, and Matt Gardner. In Proceedings of ACL-2022, pages 2736–2749.
- SpatialVLM: Endowing Vision-Language Models with Spatial Reasoning Capabilities. Chen, Boyuan and Xu, Zhuo and Kirmani, Sean and Ichter, Brian and Driess, Danny and Florence, Pete and Sadigh, Dorsa and Guibas, Leonidas and Xia, Fei,arXiv preprint arXiv:2401.12168,2024.
- Visual Spatial Reasoning. Fangyu Liu, Guy Emerson, Nigel Collier; Transactions of the Association for Computational Linguistics 2023.
- Multi-agent Motion Planning from Signal Temporal Logic Specifications. Dawei Sun, Jingkai Chen, Sayan Mitra, Chuchu Fan. IEEE Robotics and Automation Letters (RA-L).
- NL2TL: Transforming Natural Languages to Temporal Logics using Large Language Models. Yongchao Chen, Rujul Gandhi, Yang Zhang, and Chuchu Fan. Proceedings of the 2023 Conference on Empirical Methods in Natural Language Processing, 2023.

4 Instructors

- **Parisa Kordjamshidi** is an Assistant Professor of the Computer Science Department at Michigan State University. She has been working on spatial semantics extraction and annotation schemes, mapping language to formal spatial representations, spatial ontologies, structured output prediction models for information extraction, and combining vision and language for spatial language understanding. She has organized/co-organized shared tasks on Spatial role labeling, SpRL-2012, SpRL-2013, and the Space Evaluation workshop, SpaceEval-2015, in the SemEval Series and Multimodal spatial role labeling workshop mSpRL at CLEF-2017 intending to consider vision and language media for spatial information extraction. She organized SpLU at (NAACL-18, EMNLP-2020) and Robonlp-SpLU at (NAACL-2019, ACL-IJCNLP 2021). Email: kordjams@msu.edu. Webpage: `http://www.cse.msu.edu/~kordjams`.

- **Qiang Ning** is an applied scientist at AWS (2022-) leading the human alignment team for Titan LLMs. Prior to that, Qiang was an applied scientist at Alexa (2020-2022) and a research scientist at the Allen Institute for AI (2019-2020). Qiang received his Ph.D. from the University of Illinois at Urbana-Champaign in 2019 in Electrical and Computer Engineering. Qiang's research interests span in information extraction, question answering, and the application of weak supervision methods in these NLP problems in both theoretical and practical aspects. Email: qiangning.01@gmail.com. Webpage: `https://www.qiangning.info/`

- **James Pustejovsky** is the TJX Feldberg Chair in Computer Science at Brandeis University, where he is also Chair of the Linguistics Program, Chair of the Computational Linguistics MA Program, and Director of the Lab for Linguistics and Computation. He received his B.S. from MIT and his Ph.D. from UMASS at Amherst. He has worked on computational and lexical semantics for 25 years and is the chief developer of Generative Lexicon Theory. Since 2002, he has been working on the development of a platform for temporal reasoning in language, called TARSQI (www.tarsqi.org). Pustejovsky is the chief architect of TimeML and ISO-TimeML, a recently adopted ISO standard for temporal information in language, as well as the recently adopted standard, ISO-Space, a specification for spatial information in language. He has developed a modeling framework for representing linguistic expressions and interactions as multimodal simulations. This platform, VoxML, enables real-time communication between humans and computers or robots for joint tasks, utilizing speech, gesture, gaze, and action. He is currently working with robotics researchers in HRI to allow the VoxML platform to act as both a dialogue management system as well as a simulation environment that reveals real-time epistemic state and perceptual input to a computational agent. His areas of interest include Computational semantics, temporal and spatial reasoning, language annotation for machines. Email: jamesp@brandeis.edu. Webpage: `http://www.pusto.com`.

- **Marie-Francine Moens** is a Full Professor at the Department of Computer Science, KU Leuven. She has a special interest in machine learning for natural language understanding and in grounding language in a visual context. She is a holder of the prestigious ERC Advanced Grant CALCULUS (2018-2023) granted by the European Research Council on the topic of language understanding. She is currently associate editor of the journal IEEE Transactions on Pattern Analysis and Machine Intelligence (TPAMI). In 2011 and 2012 she was appointed as chair of the European Chapter of the Association for Computational Linguistics (EACL) and was a member of the executive board of the Association for Computational Linguistics (ACL). From 2014 to 2018 she was the scientific manager of the EU COST action iV&L Net (The European Network on Integrating Vision and Language). Email: sien.moens@cs.kuleuven.be. Webpage: `https://people.cs.kuleuven.be/~sien.moens`

References

Malihe Alikhani and Matthew Stone. 2020. Achieving common ground in multi-modal dialogue. In *Proceedings of the 58th Annual Meeting of the Association for Computational Linguistics: Tutorial Abstracts*, pages 10–15.

James F Allen. 1984. Towards a general theory of action and time. *Artificial Intelligence*, 23(2):123–154.

Piyush Bagad, Makarand Tapaswi, and Cees G.M. Snoek. 2023. Test of time: Instilling video-language models with a sense of time. In *2023 IEEE/CVF Conference on Computer Vision and Pattern Recognition (CVPR)*, pages 2503–2516.

Yejin Bang, Samuel Cahyawijaya, Nayeon Lee, Wenliang Dai, Dan Su, Bryan Wilie, Holy Lovenia, Ziwei Ji, Tiezheng Yu, Willy Chung, Quyet V. Do, Yan Xu, and Pascale Fung. 2023. A multitask, multilingual, multimodal evaluation of chatgpt on reasoning, hallucination, and interactivity.

J. A. Bateman. 2010. Language and space: A two-level semantic approach based on principles of ontological engineering. *International Journal of Speech Technology*, 13(1):29–48.

Nathanael Chambers, Taylor Cassidy, Bill McDowell, and Steven Bethard. 2014. Dense event ordering with a multi-pass architecture. 2:273–284.

Boyuan Chen, Zhuo Xu, Sean Kirmani, Brian Ichter, Danny Driess, Pete Florence, Dorsa Sadigh, Leonidas Guibas, and Fei Xia. 2024. Spatialvlm: Endowing vision-language models with spatial reasoning capabilities.

Jaemin Cho, Abhay Zala, and Mohit Bansal. 2023. Dall-eval: Probing the reasoning skills and social biases of text-to-image generation models. In *Proceedings of the IEEE/CVF International Conference on Computer Vision (ICCV)*, pages 3043–3054.

Anthony G. Cohn, Brandon Bennett, John Gooday, and Nicholas M. Gotts. 1997. Representing and reasoning with qualitative spatial relations. In Oliviero Stock, editor, *Spatial and Temporal Reasoning*, pages 97–132. Springer.

Guillem Collell, Thierry Deruyttere, and Marie-Francine Moens. 2021. Probing spatial clues: Canonical spatial templates for object relationship understanding. *IEEE Access*, 9:134298–134318.

Soham Dan, Parisa Kordjamshidi, Julia Bonn, Archna Bhatia, Martha Palmer, and Dan Roth. 2020. In *Proceedings of Language Resources and Evaluation Conference, LREC-2020*.

Liesbeth Degand and Philippe Muller. 2020. Dialogue and dialogue systems. *TAL: revue internationale Traitement Automatique des Langues*, 61(3).

Thierry Deruyttere, Victor Milewski, and Marie-Francine Moens. 2021. Giving commands to a self-driving car: How to deal with uncertain situations? *Eng. Appl. Artif. Intell.*, 103:104257.

Hao Fei, Shengqiong Wu, Wei Ji, Hanwang Zhang, and Tat-Seng Chua. 2023. Empowering dynamics-aware text-to-video diffusion with large language models.

Jonathan Francis, Nariaki Kitamura, Felix Labelle, Xiaopeng Lu, Ingrid Navarro, and Jean Oh. 2021. Core challenges in embodied vision-language planning.

Dusan Grujicic, Thierry Deruyttere, Marie-Francine Moens, and Matthew B. Blaschko. 2022. Predicting physical world destinations for commands given to self-driving cars. In *Thirty-Sixth AAAI Conference on Artificial Intelligence, AAAI 2022, Thirty-Fourth Conference on Innovative Applications of Artificial Intelligence, IAAI 2022, The Twelveth Symposium on Educational Advances in Artificial Intelligence, EAAI 2022 Virtual Event, February 22 - March 1, 2022*, pages 715–725. AAAI Press.

Rujun Han, I-Hung Hsu, Jiao Sun, Julia Baylon, Qiang Ning, Dan Roth, and Nanyun Peng. 2021. ESTER: A Machine Reading Comprehension Dataset for Reasoning about Event Semantic Relations. In *Proc. of the Conference on Empirical Methods in Natural Language Processing (EMNLP)*.

Johana Hois and Oliver Kutz. 2011. Towards linguistically-grounded spatial logics. In *Spatial Representation and Reasoning in Language: Ontologies and Logics of Space*, number 10131 in Dagstuhl Seminar Proceedings. Schloss Dagstuhl - Leibniz-Zentrum fuer Informatik, Germany.

Ronghang Hu, Jacob Andreas, Marcus Rohrbach, Trevor Darrell, and Kate Saenko. 2017. Learning to reason: End-to-end module networks for visual question answering. *2017 IEEE International Conference on Computer Vision (ICCV)*, pages 804–813.

Ronghang Hu, Daniel Fried, Anna Rohrbach, Dan Klein, Trevor Darrell, and Kate Saenko. 2019. Are you looking? grounding to multiple modalities in vision-and-language navigation. In *Proceedings of the 57th Conference of the Association for Computational Linguistics, ACL 2019, Florence, Italy, July 28- August 2, 2019, Volume 1: Long Papers*, pages 6551–6557.

Drew A Hudson and Christopher D Manning. 2018. Compositional attention networks for machine reasoning. In *International Conference on Learning Representations (ICLR)*.

Drew A Hudson and Christopher D Manning. 2019. GQA: A new dataset for real-world visual reasoning and compositional question answering. *Conference on Computer Vision and Pattern Recognition (CVPR)*.

T. Kollar, S. Tellex, D. Roy, and N. Roy. 2010. Toward understanding natural language directions. In *Proceeding of the 5th ACM/IEEE International Conference on Human-Robot Interaction*, HRI '10, pages 259–266. ACM.

Parisa Kordjamshidi and Marie-Francine Moens. 2015. Global machine learning for spatial ontology population. *Web Semant.*, 30(C):3–21.

Parisa Kordjamshidi, Martijn van Otterlo, and Marie-Francine Moens. 2010. Spatial role labeling: task definition and annotation scheme. In *Proceedings of the Seventh Conference on International Language Resources and Evaluation (LREC'10)*, pages 413–420.

Parisa Kordjamshidi, Martijn van Otterlo, and Marie-Francine Moens. 2011. Spatial role labeling: towards extraction of spatial relations from natural language. *ACM - Transactions on Speech and Language Processing*, 8:1–36.

Parisa Kordjamshidi, Martijn van Otterlo, and Marie-Francine Moens. 2017. Spatial role labeling annotation scheme. In N. Ide James Pustejovsky, editor, *Handbook of Linguistic Annotation*. Springer Verlag.

Katherine Krajovic, Nikhil Krishnaswamy, Nathaniel J Dimick, R Pito Salas, and James Pustejovsky. 2020. Situated multimodal control of a mobile robot: Navigation through a virtual environment. *arXiv e-prints*, pages arXiv–2007.

Nikhil Krishnaswamy, Scott Friedman, and James Pustejovsky. 2019. Combining deep learning and qualitative spatial reasoning to learn complex structures from sparse examples with noise. In *Proceedings of the thirty-third AAAI Conference on Artificial Intelligence*.

Artuur Leeuwenberg and Marie-Francine Moens. 2018. Temporal information extraction by predicting relative time-lines. In *Proceedings of the 2018 Conference on Empirical Methods in Natural Language Processing*, pages 1237–1246, Brussels, Belgium. Association for Computational Linguistics.

Artuur Leeuwenberg and Marie-Francine Moens. 2020. Towards extracting absolute event timelines from english clinical reports. *IEEE/ACM Trans. Audio, Speech and Lang. Proc.*, 28:2710–2719.

Hengli Li, Song-Chun Zhu, and Zilong Zheng. 2023. Diplomat: a dialogue dataset for situated pragmatic reasoning. *Advances in Neural Information Processing Systems*, 36:46856–46884.

Fangyu Liu, Guy Emerson, and Nigel Collier. 2023. Visual spatial reasoning. *Transactions of the Association for Computational Linguistics*, 11:635–651.

Yunchao Liu, Jiajun Wu, Zheng Wu, Daniel Ritchie, William T. Freeman, and Joshua B. Tenenbaum. 2019. Learning to describe scenes with programs. In *International Conference on Learning Representations*.

Gengchen Mai, Krzysztof Janowicz, Ling Cai, Rui Zhu, Blake Regalia, Bo Yan, Meilin Shi, and Ni Lao. 2020. Se-kge: A location-aware knowledge graph embedding model for geographic question answering and spatial semantic lifting. *Transactions in GIS*, 24(3):623–655.

I. Mani and James Pustejovsky. 2012. *Interpreting Motion: Grounded Representations for Spatial Language*. Explorations in language and space. Oxford University Press.

Inderjeet Mani. 2009. SpatialML: annotation scheme for marking spatial expression in natural language. Technical Report Version 3.0, The MITRE Corporation.

Roshanak Mirzaee, Hossein Rajaby Faghihi, Qiang Ning, and Parisa Kordjmashidi. 2021. SpartQA: A textual question answering benchmark for spatial reasoning. *NAACL*.

Roshanak Mirzaee and Parisa Kordjamshidi. 2022. Transfer learning with synthetic corpora for spatial role labeling and reasoning. In *Proceedings of the 2022 Conference on Empirical Methods in Natural Language Processing*, pages 6148–6165, Abu Dhabi, United Arab Emirates. Association for Computational Linguistics.

Aditya Mogadala, Marimuthu Kalimuthu, and Dietrich Klakow. 2021. Trends in integration of vision and language research: A survey of tasks, datasets, and methods. *J. Artif. Int. Res.*, 71:1183–1317.

Qiang Ning, Hao Wu, Rujun Han, Nanyun Peng, Matt Gardner, and Dan Roth. 2020. TORQUE: A Reading Comprehension Dataset of Temporal ORdering QUEstions. In *Proc. of the Conference on Empirical Methods in Natural Language Processing (EMNLP)*.

Qiang Ning, Hao Wu, and Dan Roth. 2018a. A multi-axis annotation scheme for event temporal relations. pages 1318–1328. Association for Computational Linguistics.

Qiang Ning, Ben Zhou, Zhili Feng, Haoruo Peng, and Dan Roth. 2018b. CogCompTime: A Tool for Understanding Time in Natural Language. In *EMNLP (Demo Track)*, Brussels, Belgium. Association for Computational Linguistics.

Qiang Ning, Ben Zhou, Hao Wu, Haoruo Peng, Chuchu Fan, and Matt Gardner. 2022. A meta-framework for spatiotemporal quantity extraction from text. In *Proceedings of the 60th Annual Meeting of the Association for Computational Linguistics (Volume 1: Long Papers)*, pages 2736–2749, Dublin, Ireland. Association for Computational Linguistics.

J. Pustejovsky, J. Castaño, R. Ingria, R. Saurí, R. Gaizauskas, A. Setzer, and G. Katz. 2003a. TimeML: Robust specification of event and temporal expressions in text. In *in Fifth International Workshop on Computational Semantics (IWCS-5)*.

James Pustejovsky. 2017. Iso-space: Annotating static and dynamic spatial information. In *Handbook of Linguistic Annotation*, pages 989–1024. Springer.

James Pustejovsky, Patrick Hanks, Roser Sauri, Andrew See, Robert Gaizauskas, Andrea Setzer, Dragomir Radev, Beth Sundheim, David Day, Lisa Ferro, et al. 2003b. The TIMEBANK corpus. In *Corpus Linguistics*, page 40.

James Pustejovsky and Nikhil Krishnaswamy. 2021. Embodied human computer interaction. *KI-Künstliche Intelligenz*, pages 1–21.

James Pustejovsky, J. Moszkowicz, and M. Verhagen. 2011. ISO-Space: The annotation of spatial information in language. In *ACL-ISO International Workshop on Semantic Annotation (ISA'6)*.

Taher Rahgooy, Umar Manzoor, and Parisa Kordjamshidi. 2018. Visually guided spatial relation extraction from text. In *Proceedings of The 16th Annual Conference of the North American Chapter of the Association for Computational Linguistics, NAACL HLT 2018*.

Zhengxiang Shi, Qiang Zhang, and Aldo Lipani. 2022. Stepgame: A new benchmark for robust multi-hop spatial reasoning in texts. In *Proceedings of the AAAI Conference on Artificial Intelligence*, volume 36, pages 11321–11329.

Kristin Stock, Robert C. Pasley, Zoe Gardner, Paul Brindley, Jeremy Morley, and Claudia Cialone. 2013. Creating a corpus of geospatial natural language. In *Spatial Information Theory*, pages 279–298, Cham. Springer International Publishing.

Alane Suhr, Mike Lewis, James Yeh, and Yoav Artzi. 2017. A corpus of natural language for visual reasoning. In *ACL*.

Alane Suhr, Stephanie Zhou, Iris Zhang, Huajun Bai, and Yoav Artzi. 2018. A corpus for reasoning about natural language grounded in photographs. *arXiv preprint arXiv:1811.00491*.

S. Tellex, T. Kollar, S. Dickerson, M. R. Walter, A. G. Banerjee, S. Teller, and N. Roy. 2011. Understanding natural language commands for robotic navigation and mobile manipulation. In *Proceedings of the National Conference on Artificial Intelligence (AAAI)*.

Jesse Thomason, Jivko Sinapov, Raymond Mooney, and Peter Stone. 2018. Guiding exploratory behaviors for multi-modal grounding of linguistic descriptions. In *Proceedings of the Thirty-Second AAAI Conference on Artificial Intelligence (AAAI-18)*.

Ruben Villegas, Mohammad Babaeizadeh, Pieter-Jan Kindermans, Hernan Moraldo, Han Zhang, Mohammad Taghi Saffar, Santiago Castro, Julius Kunze, and Dumitru Erhan. 2022. Phenaki: Variable length video generation from open domain textual description.

Yue Zhang, Quan Guo, and Parisa Kordjamshidi. 2024. NavHint: Vision and language navigation agent with a hint generator. In *Findings of the Association for Computational Linguistics: EACL 2024*, pages 92–103, St. Julian's, Malta. Association for Computational Linguistics.

Yue Zhang and Parisa Kordjamshidi. Vln-trans, translator for the vision and language navigation agent. *The 61st Annual Meeting of the Association for Computational Linguistics (ACL-2023)*.

Kaiyu Zheng, Deniz Bayazit, Rebecca Mathew, Ellie Pavlick, and Stefanie Tellex. 2021. Spatial language understanding for object search in partially observed city-scale environments.

Author Index